Self Helping

Dr. Scott Alpert

DEDICATION

This book is dedicated to the memory of Ray Bradbury who was a mentor and a friend.

THE CONTENTS

INTRODUCTION

"Finish each day and be done with it. You have done what you could. Some blunders and absurdities no doubt crept in; forget them as soon as you can. Tomorrow is a new day. You shall begin it serenely and with too high a spirit to be encumbered with your old nonsense." — **Ralph Waldo Emerson**

Treating debilitating problems without the proper knowhow can be difficult if not impossible. When you are educated on how to use your innate ability to heal, problems are merely invitations for growth and healing.

This book can be a great resource whether you suffer from undue stress, addiction, mood problems, and physical ailments, or if you have simply given up on life. Instead of covering up problems with a BAND AID®, get ready to learn how to remove problems right from their root.

My name is Dr. Scott Alpert and since 1994 I have been treating people using a combination of Psychology and Spirituality. I believe that the best teachers are those who have been there, done that, and got the t-shirt for it - which describes me.

In treating thousands of people, I have dealt with a wide assortment of problems, so know that you are in good hands. I will be providing some real-life examples that will help you relate more easily to your own problems as you and I go on this adventure together. And this is going to be an adventure into the heart of you.

If you've never gone through therapy, generally, two people - a therapist and a client - open themselves up, look at the difficulties the client is going through, and then create a plan of action. If you are willing to follow the steps in this book, you can literally plot your own plan of action and counsel yourself. All it takes is a willingness on your part to continually stretch and grow and keep moving forward. And trust me, healing yourself is mostly a labor of love.

How are you with you? Is it common for you to get drawn into the problems of others? Do you get trapped in your own negativity, anger and despair? Do you feel like there is no hope and no way out? Have you given up?

Statistics

One in five people in the United States have a serious mental health condition or addictive habit that warrants professional treatment. Millions are suffering, unaware of how to improve.

Beneficial mental health treatment addresses the mental level, physical behaviors, and the emotions. Unfortunately, most people are treated with "Medication Management", where the symptoms are treated but not the root cause. Getting to the root of a problem will provide you the best results. Yet few therapists are trained to do so.

Getting proper help can be difficult. There are serious financial, time, and logistical constraints, and finding an expert that takes your insurance or what you can afford can feel like an impossibility. Still miracles do happen.

According to Psychiatry.com, in 2011, Panic attacks attributed to 1.2 million emergency room visits. These visits were emotionally based and caused physical symptoms. We are interconnected physically, mentally, emotionally, and spiritually, treating our whole-self increases the odds of success.

Here are some questions for you to ponder. What percentage of your thoughts are positive? How is your physical body? How is your relationship with you? How is your relationship with God? Be honest with yourself since you are about to go on an exploration of all this and more and facing the reality of the situation is essential.

Let's make a pact right now and read this book sober. Having a few drinks, a few pills, or a few hits will impair your ability to process this information clearly. Plus, the point of this book is healing yourself anyway. Why not do this 100 percent?

Many argue that having a cigarette, smoking pot, or having a drink keeps them calm. According to the National Institute on Drug Abuse, long term Cannabis use affects your IQ and memory and creates depression. In addition, the U.S. National Library on Medicine (2013) stated that cigarette smoking has been associated with increased anxiety and anxiety disorders. Alcohol is a depressant that causes damage to the organs and brain. Give yourself the opportunity to better yourself without the damage.

Mahatma Gandhi used to travel around India in a private train when he retired. People used to line up to meet with him and a woman entered with a teen aged boy, upset that he was eating too much sugar. No matter how much she lectured her son, he continued to eat it. She felt it made him lazy and it contributed to him not doing anything with his life. At her wits end she brought her son to meet with Gandhi.

Gandhi listened to the woman carefully, turned and then spoke to her,

"Go home and come back in two weeks."
The woman looked perplexed and wondered why he had not told her son to stop eating sugar but left. Two weeks later she returned with her son.

Gandhi looked directly at the boy and said,

"Boy, you should stop eating sugar. It is not good for your health."

The boy nodded and promised he would not continue this habit any longer.

The boy's mother turned to Gandhi and asked,

"Why didn't you tell him that two weeks ago when I brought him here to see you?"

Gandhi smiled,

"Because two weeks ago I was eating sugar myself."

Notice

This book is intended to educate and not treat you. Think of this as a scholastic text. Yes, there is going to be detailed descriptions of psychological methods, there will be homework, extra credit assignments, and pop quizzes… just kidding. However, homework exercises will be provided, so please complete them for one reason: they are meant to help you improve. Reading information is good but putting the knowledge into action can be life altering. Professional assistance is always recommended.

CHAPTER ONE: LET'S BEGIN OUR JOURNEY

"The journey of a thousand miles begins with one step." - **Lao Tzu**

Trial and Error

We learn through trial and error. It took a lot of falling before you learned how to walk. If you aren't failing, you aren't growing. How you handle failure is the issue. Problems inevitably take place but befriending yourself in the process of failing keeps your relationship with you positive which is the key to emotional wellbeing.

The way we treat ourselves when we are going through a problem mimics the way our family of origin did. If they took a drink, avoided talking about problems, and blamed others, you probably do the same. Problems, however, can be used as opportunities for healing and growth, if you are willing to do the work.

Two Wolves

An Indian Chief gathered all the children of the tribe for a talk about life. He confesses: "There is a battle that goes on inside of my head. It is like a battle between two wolves. One wolf is evil. It is angry, envious, jealous, filled with sorrow, regret, greed, arrogance, self-pity, guilt, resentment, inferiority, lies, false pride, superiority, and ego. The other wolf however is good. It is filled with joy, peace, love, hope, serenity, humility, kindness, benevolence, empathy, generosity, truth, compassion, and faith."

The children thought about it for a minute and then one asked, "Which wolf wins?"

The Chief simply replied, "the one that I feed."

Which wolf do you feed? Are you more negative than positive? In training your mind to focus on the glass being half-full, you create a healthier outlook, a healthier body, a clearer mind, and more inner peace.

> *"A negative attitude drains, a positive attitude energizes."* — **Lindsey Rietzsch**

Emotional Bank Account

Opening your heart to yourself is how the healing process begins. Be a friend to you. Catch yourself doing something right. Pat yourself on the back for a job well done. As you do so, you are making deposits into your emotional bank account.

We were taught to please others so they could please us. Avoiding the middleman is a better strategy. When you don't care for yourself it is more difficult to care for others.

Punishing yourself when you fail doesn't make things better, it only keeps you trapped in misery. You cannot hurt yourself enough to make something better. Negative plus negative still equals negative. If you did something "wrong", learn from it, make the adjustments, acknowledge yourself for learning the lesson, and then make it "right" the next time.

In childhood we were trained to punish ourselves for not measuring up properly. It is okay for you to stop doing this behavior. When you learn from your errors, they can be viewed as stepping stones to the current and improved you.

*My fiancé walked in the kitchen and began to pick a fight.
She was angry because she remembered something I did
in the past that made her upset. Refusing to get drawn
into an argument, I held onto my good mood and replied,
"Yep, that sounds like something I would have done a few
years ago and I am so grateful I have learned from it."*

The Destination

As with any journey, it is important to first have a destination,
otherwise you will be meandering around aimlessly.

What is your goal? What do you want to get out of reading this
book? What do you want to get out of life? An "Intention" starts
the process to achieving it.

Intentions basically put your desires into motion. It's as if you tell
yourself, "This is what I want, and I am now stepping in the
direction toward it."

You set intentions all the time without even knowing it. "Today is
going to be shitty". In other words, you are saying, "My intention
is to make this a shitty day" and of course the day gets more and
more shitty. Why not create a good experience? If you wake up
feeling sick, set an intention to feel well. "My intention is to feel
better." Then take the proper action steps to create wellness.

*"The power of intention is the power to manifest, to
create, to live a life of unlimited abundance, and to
attract into your life the right people at the right
moments."* - **Wayne Dyer**

Exercise: Intention Setting

Take a moment to jot down a series of intentions for the remainder
of the day.

To create an intention, follow this format:

"My intention is _____". It is really that simple.

For example: "My intention is to be gentle and easy on myself."

Another example: "My intention is to heal."

Setting an intention before anything you do creates "Mindfulness" - Mindfulness is being in a state of loving awareness.

At the beginning of each day, recite a series of intentions. Recite intentions before any social interaction. Set intentions before driving. Set intentions before going to sleep. Each day can be broken into segments. Set intentions before each segment to take control over your life.

> *I was treating a woman who was severely abused as a child. Her intention was to give love to the infant part of her that went thorough horror. Each session, she hugged a pillow and rocked back and forth while crying. When the hour was up, she wiped her tears, thanked me and left. After a month of this routine, she said she felt healed and discharged.*

With a clear intention, mountains can move. Riding herself of the horrors of the past was this woman's mountain.

You cannot intend for others. For example, "My intention is for him to love me". Efforts to manipulate the external will fail. To have results externally, change internally. This will create a magnet for the same energy to come back to you. When you are down, people kick you. When you are up, people adore you.

Write down a minimum of two intentions before continuing with the reading.

My intention is:

My intention is:

Clean Slate

It is important to view each day as having a fresh start. You can choose to drag the past with you if you want or learn from the past and move forward. "Lesson learned." It is important for you to judge yourself by your current actions and avoid hanging a label on yourself of your past deeds. Your current self is the real you. What you did in the past is all you could have done with the information you had back then and how you were feeling physically, mentally, and emotionally at the time. In understanding you are doing the very best you can in any given moment, it is easier to let go of the self-judgement. Remember that life is all about trial and error. You tried something, it failed, you learned, and are moving forward. It is important to view yourself and others as you currently are.

> *"The past is history, the future a mystery, but now is a gift - that is why it is called the present."* –
> **Anonymous**

It is common to drag the past with us. For example, when a person says, "I always have difficulties with _____" they are saying, "My intention is to continue to have difficulties with _____." However, in saying, "Up to this point I have had difficulties with _____" you are giving your consciousness a breaking-off point. Up to this point, means, "In the past I have had a problem with _____, but now I have the opportunity to be different." You can change. Listen to the words that you say. If you say something that locks in old thinking patterns, change them quickly. As you work on yourself, you will become more aware of what you are telling yourself and others. If an old habitual pattern leaks out, quickly reword it.

Baby Steps

Emotions have a language all their own. It's more hands on and touchy feely than problem solving. Many feel they would rather die than face their emotions. A bit extreme wouldn't you think?

However, I've heard this often with recovering addicts. A past girlfriend of mine used to say, "You don't need to pole vault over mouse turds". An interesting quote but this is true. It is surprising to discover that when you really face your emotions, they really aren't so high in the sky. Just keep breathing. You will be okay. If you don't face them, emotional wounds left untreated tend to become more and more severe.

> *I was visiting my grandmother at her old age home, when another resident started sobbing. I sat down next to her to lend assistance. She had remembered something her father did 90 years earlier and it was still upsetting her.*

Rest assured we are first going to take baby steps before diving into deep emotional wounds. Think of emotional work as slowly wading into a swimming pool from the shallow end. First you will get comfortable with the water and find your feet. Then step by step you will get a few strokes mastered, swim about and when you enter the deeper waters you will be well prepared to deep-sea dive.

The first baby step is learning how to apply love to your hurt. This love is not from another person, but by you loving you. *When you apply love to hurt you heal*. This is a revolutionary model from Spiritual Psychology. No rituals, no fancy prayers, no chanting, it is simply grabbing hold of the part inside of you that went through a difficult situation and providing love to this tender part. Your task, from now to the end of this book and beyond is to be kind to yourself. Remind yourself that you are a good person and your intention is to be a loving ally. Do the little things that shows you care about you. Place Post-It® notes around your home reminding you about how wonderful you are. Keep repeating in your mind that you can and are changing for the better. Above all, treat yourself with kindness.

As you lay the groundwork for the upcoming emotional work at the deeper end of the pool, a different relationship with yourself will start to emerge. One that is more confident and more trusting of you. Many clients state that as they start to work on improving their relationship with themselves, they feel that they have their own back and trust themselves – maybe for the first time. How wonderful it is to know that somebody is always there for you and that person *is you*.

Emotional problems strike at our heart. They can be disabling. According to Fritz Perls[1] from Gestalt Therapy[2,3], when we go through a traumatic experience, a portion of us gets emotionally stuck there. This is the reason why people have repeated memories of difficult situations they went through because their mind is still grappling with it. However, in learning to surround yourself in love and love the part of you that went through that ordeal, you heal! Healing is an act of love!

> *"What lies behind you and what lies in front of you, pales in comparison to what lies inside of you."* –
> **Ralph Waldo Emerson**

Review

- We learn through trial and error.
- We discussed the *two wolves*.
- Intention setting helps you take initial steps towards your goal. What are your intentions for:
  - Reading this book?
  - Your day?
  - The next hour?
- The importance of creating a loving relationship with yourself.
- Catching yourself doing something right.
- Making the commitment to support you.

Notes:

CHAPTER TWO: INTERNAL VOWS

"The life you have left is a gift. Cherish it. Enjoy it now, to the fullest. Do what matters, now." — **Leo Babauta**

The Number One Priority

The only person that can get you through difficult times is you. You can change your life for the better if you make yourself the top priority. Making yourself the number one priority has been labeled Narcissistic or just plain wrong. When you make others or obligations more important than you, what is the meta-message you are telling yourself?

When you make others the priority, you avoid yourself, drain your battery, and limit your potential. If you instead took the effort to care for your own needs first, it eliminates the middle person and makes healing more attainable.

I attended a seminar in which we married ourselves. I literally got a ring, got down on my knee, and made vows that I still try to keep to this day. I learned that in any relationship, especially with our relationship with ourselves, commitment is important.

I am Upset

Does this statement look familiar? "I am upset *because* _____."

Let's break this down. "I am upset" means - I feel upset inside of myself. "Because" means - something externally happened and mentally I am choosing to think of it as upsetting.

When the actions of another person upset you, they don't make you feel upset, you do. Our brain works so fast that we believe other people's actions directly make us feel a certain way, but we did. When something happens outside of us, it goes through our filter and we label it as good or bad and then attach an emotion to it.

When you focus your efforts on changing the them, you can expect little to no success. In focusing your efforts on healing your own upset, this is how we improve. The only person you can change is you. You cannot change others. It is not your job. You control you, they control them. No matter how great you think you are at manipulating people, others are always going to be themselves. *You have direct impact on your thoughts, feelings, and actions, and are in control over your life!* Focus on taking care of your upset. Regardless if you believe you are right and they are wrong, you still had a reaction and that reaction came from you. Because you caused it, you can change it.

> *"No one can make you successful; the will to success comes from within. I've made this my motto. I've internalized it to the point of understanding that the success of my actions and/or endeavors doesn't depend on anyone else, and that includes a possible failure."* - **Fabrizio Moreira**

> *In a PBS Radio interview, George Harrison from The Beatles, talked about the mayhem with "Beatlemania". He said, when people got caught up in the insanity of Beatlemania, they literally went mad. Four silly guys were enclosed in a limousine having the times of their lives and all around them the world was going crazy!*

As you move away from focusing on other peoples' actions and focus on your own, you can create the eye of the hurricane within you. This is at the heart of true self-care.

"In the long run, we shape our lives, and we shape ourselves. The process never ends until we die. And the choices we make are ultimately our own responsibility." — **Eleanor Roosevelt**

Meditation

"The thing about meditation: You become more and more you" – **David Lynch**

Meditation creates a deeper connection with yourself, your life, and the God of your understanding. Tune out the world and tune in to you.

To meditate, simply sit quietly and breathe. Allow your mind to go blank. There is nothing you need to do at this moment; this moment is just for you. Feel your radiance. What a gift you have been given – this body, this life, the ability to think, to feel, to love. Open your heart to you.

Meditation is great for mind, body, emotions, and spirit. It allows you to slow down and simply be. It is the perfect antidote to a busy lifestyle. The body and brain need rest to repair. When the mind is constantly going, it moves you further away from peace.

To take meditation to the next level, connect with the rhythm of your breathing. If any thoughts come to mind, simply observe them, breathe in, and with an exhale let them go. Give yourself permission to be at peace.

If during your meditation, you have recurring thoughts, this is referred to as the Visitor. Jot down recurring thoughts and later deal with them. For now, simply breathe and feel life flowing within you.

After 10 minutes of meditation, continue with the reading.

Self-Appreciation

Improving your relationship with yourself is needed to create a solid foundation for wellbeing. Your relationship with yourself improves through "Self-Appreciation" which can be thought of as "catching yourself doing something right." How often do you appreciate your own efforts? Here is a cute little format to remind yourself about how wonderful you are. Simply state:

"I appreciate myself for _____"

Here are a few examples:

"I appreciate myself for reading this book."

"I appreciate myself for meditating 10 minutes."

"I appreciate myself for hugging my innermost self."

"I appreciate myself for having an open mind."

It may feel good when other people praise you, but when you truly praise yourself it can be profound.

On a trip to Taos New Mexico, my back went out. No longer able to ski, I asked myself what I wanted to do. I ended up at a great hotel next to the Grand Canyon. I went to an incredible place for dinner and while reading the menu it dawned on me - I had always asked dates to order whatever they wanted and kept myself to a strict budget. This evening I ordered the best meal and when it arrived, I started to cry. I never made myself the number-one priority before. I overheard a family at the next table talking about the incredible helicopter ride they went on, so the next morning I went on the same flight. This was the first time I made peace with myself.

"Then I Love Me!"

I was with a friend and her four-year-old granddaughter. I asked little Hannah who she loved.

"Well," she said with a smile, "I love Nanna and Poppa, and Auntie Kimmie, and uncle Ken, and Mommy, and you," she said with an impish grin.

"What about you?" I asked.

"Oh no", she replied. "People aren't supposed to love themselves!"

"Why not?" I asked. "If you don't love yourself, how can you love others?"

Suddenly she stopped and pondered the statement, and then smiled, "Then I love me!"

Her grandmother and I laughed.

When her mother walked into the room, Hannah rushed to her.

"Mommy, Mommy, I love me," she smiled wide.

Her mother looked at me and said furiously – "Scott!"

From an early age, we were taught to only give away our love to others and it was wrong to love us. Is it really that wrong to love and nurture ourselves? At 99 years old, my grandmother asked me if I cracked myself up like she always did. Throughout my grandmother's entire 99 years she had a fun-filled relationship with her. You are with you 24/7 and from this point there are two paths you can walk – one is befriending you and the other is being harsh. Which path do you choose?

New Eyes

J. Kristnamurti[4], who created the Ojai Foundation, in Ojai California, had a principle: "See things with new eyes". If we were not swayed by our past beliefs and saw people as they were, he believed we saw the truth. An enemy could become a close friend, a close friend could stab us in the back.

Try to see a person just as they are. You are not obligated to be their friend for life. As my sister Kim says, "people come into your life for a reason, a season, or for a lifetime".

"If you choose bad companions, no one will believe that you are anything but bad yourself." — **Aesop**

Review

- Make yourself the number one priority.
- We went over the I am upset, because _____ model
- We discussed moving away from controlling the world and simply controlling yourself.
- We looked at self-care processes which include the following:
    - Meditation,
    - Self-appreciation, and
    - Self-love.

Notes:

CHAPTER THREE: UNFINISHED BUSINESS

"Life can only be understood backward; but it must be lived forwards." — **Søren Kierkegaard**

Riding an Issue Back in Time

Until the wounds from your past are addressed, it is natural for them to come to mind, play out in your dreams, or repeat themselves. This is the mind's way of trying to make sense of what happened and put the problem to rest. "Out of sight out of mind" and "words will never harm me" are wonderful idioms and fairy tales, but the deeper meaning is, "out of sight, into subconscious mind" and "words can break our heart in two."

When you have a reaction to an event, observe your feeling, hold onto it, and ride it back in time to when you first recall feeling that way originally. Here lays the root of the problem. Once you find the root, the healing cycle can begin.

Love Applied to Hurt

Riding feelings back in time brings you smack dab to you at a younger age. When you lovingly interact with your wounded younger self, emotional problems can heal. Many people shy away from the idea of doing this because they don't want to experience the pain again. Yes, this process brings hurt feelings to the surface, but this type of healing is done in a different way. Instead of focusing on the event, focus on the younger you that went through the difficulty. This puts into action the model - *When love is applied to hurt, you heal.*

When Spiritual Psychology[5] created this model, it was revolutionary. Though simple in its make-up, it is profound. It was discovered that when problems were healed at the root, every similar problem healed as well. It was like a line of energy was simply erased!

Our mind will recreate difficult situations subconsciously to make sense of our unresolved issues. Spiritual Psychology believes that if a person doesn't address a problem, it will get attracted again and again in order for the issue to be properly taken care of. The upset you feel when somebody bothers you, is basically the same bother you have experienced countless times before. In addressing this problem at the root ultimately releases this pattern.

The Spiritual Psychology approach incorporates many psychological approaches that bring the core of an issue to the surface. When the root is exposed, love becomes the healing agent!

According to Sigmund Freud[6] the father of Psychoanalysis, "regression" is a process in which under stress we revert to an earlier age-stage. Spiritual Psychology views this process as our innate method of getting to the core of a wound.

As most conventional treatment medicates, encourages one to cope with, and distract ourselves from the problem, it can hamper success. We live in a quick-fix society, which is why many people turn to substances and psychiatric medication. When this doesn't work, and all other methods fail, many people commit suicide.

When I worked at the Mental Health Urgent Care Center in Long Beach, California, our job was to treat people who were suicidal. About 90 percent of the people who were suicidal reported that they suffered from childhood abuse and had never addressed it. When young, we don't have the capacity to understand how to deal with problems because our brains don't initially wire until we are around the age of eight. Children, not having the capacity to deal with traumatic events will stuff down problems into the subconscious mind, which becomes a storehouse of unprocessed material that, as we age, starts to work its way to the surface.

Have you ever tried to hold a ball under water? Because of the pressure of the water, the opposing force wants to pop up the ball. Like the water, our subconscious mind wants to pop up emotional wounds to the surface to clear them out. It takes a lot of psychological effort to hold things down leading to exhaustion – a major component of depression.

I find myself telling people the same thing: "You are not having a break down you are having a breakthrough! You just have no more room left to store your subconscious material into and it is time to do some house cleaning". Think of all the traumatic events you have suffered and stuffed inside. Don't you think it's time to address them?

Subconscious Material

As you begin the process of healing yourself, unresolved issues will begin to surface form your sub-conscious mind. Look upon this as beneficial. These issues may have been sitting dormant for years. As you process through them, you create more internal peace and tranquility. As you honor each issue that comes to mind, befriend the part of you that went through that experience. This is how we heal – through the act of compassion towards self. Put your whole self into the process. Especially your mental and emotional selves.

Many people have suffered some horrific experiences. If this describes you, wouldn't it be incredible, at the time the experience happened, somebody rushing in and taking ultimate care of you? To truly heal, you need to be that person rushing in and providing that loving help to yourself. Wouldn't you do anything to assist the younger part inside of you that suffered? This approach can be mastered. In learning how to open your heart to the hurt parts inside of you, healing takes place!

"My scars remind me that I did indeed survive my deepest wounds. That in itself is an accomplishment. And they bring to mind something else, too. They remind me that the damage life has

inflicted on me has, in many places, left me stronger and more resilient. What hurt me in the past has actually made me better equipped to face the present." — **Steve Goodier**

Gestalt Therapy

According to Fritz Perls[1] of Gestalt Therapy, when we suffered trauma, we got emotionally stuck at that moment in time. Dr. Perls maintained, a person needed to experience a traumatic situation fully in order to learn and grow from it. Unfortunately, people shut down at times of trauma and create "unfinished business". To complete unfinished business, Dr. Perls says a past trauma needs to be viewed from as many angles as possible in order to get the full picture of the situation.

As we step outside of our own point of view and see a situation from a different perspective, insight can be gained, thus completing the business. Spiritual Psychology takes this a step further through the application of love to the part inside of you that suffered hurt.

"What happens when people open their hearts? They get better." — **Haruki Murakami**

Opposite Hand Writing

'Opposite Hand Writing[7]' allows you to, on paper, perform the Gestalt process. Allow your dominant hand to represent one perspective and your opposite hand to represent another. This is especially effective for communicating with the younger part inside of you that went through difficulty. On a piece of paper, allow your opposite hand to give voice to the younger you and your dominant hand represents you now. When the older you provides love to the 'younger you', you heal yourself!

Exercise: Opposite Hand Writing

Write out a simple conversation with the younger you. During the conversation, send love at every opportunity. Allow your younger self to complete unfinished business by getting things off his or her chest. Next, find out what the 'younger you' needs from you to feel better. Your younger self knows exactly what it needs to heal. After the request is made, do your best to fulfill these needs.

Example of Opposite Hand Writing

When I was in graduate school, I wrote this out when I was having a panic attack:

Adult: What's going on?
Child: I'm afraid.
Adult: Afraid? Why are you afraid?
Child: That teacher, she is mean and going to hurt me.
Adult: I'm not going to let her hurt you.
Child: I don't trust you.
Adult: Why don't you trust me?
Child: Because you never pay attention to me. It is all work and school and life has been a drag.
Adult: You are right. I am sorry, I promise to hang out more with you.
Child: We'll see.
Adult: I promise.
Child: Okay.
Adult: Why do you think the teacher is going to hurt you?
Child: She reminds me of the teacher in the 5th grade.
Adult: I don't remember that.
Child: Oh yeah, she made me feel stupid in front of the whole class.
Adult: I still don't remember. But I promise that I won't let the teacher hurt you. What do you want that would make you feel better?
Child: I want to run in the hallway and slide on the waxed

floor like I used to in grammar school.
Adult: Well, were in class right now. Can we do this at the
break?
Child: Okay.
Adult: Do we have to slide? I don't think my dress
pants will survive.
Child: Okay. Let's just run.
Adult: You've got a deal.
At break time I was a running fool. I am sure my fellow
students thought I had lost my mind. Still, it did the trick
and when I returned to class, I had a sense of peace.

"After a while the middle-aged person who lives in her head begins to talk to her soul, the kid." —
Anne Lamott, Joe Jones

Object Relations Therapy

Object Relations Therapy[8,9,10,11,12,13,14,15,16,17] was created by Anna Freud, Sigmund Freud's daughter. Anna Freud took a concept that her father had mentioned about the importance of social bonding in a person's life. Anna paid close attention to the mother-child bond. If this bond wasn't well established, life-long problems resulted. The goal of the therapist was to create an initial bond with the client, thereby giving them a "corrective emotional experience." In performing the Opposite Hand Writing with your youngest self, you are establishing a "Self-Bond" that leads to incredible healing.

According to the Object Relations Theory, all mental illness has its roots in early childhood experiences. Enter Spiritual Psychology: Spiritual Psychology helps people take the younger part of their personality by the hand and create a loving relationship, thereby creating the foundation for emotional wellbeing.

Visualization: Neighborhood of Your Youth

A visualization exercise is basically creating a mental movie in your mind. It is important to find a comfortable place to relax in and be undisturbed for the next 15 minutes. Visualization works best when you are relaxed, so I am including a five to one method of relaxation to begin the process.

When you are ready gently close your eyes, take in a deep relaxing breath, and exhale. Take in one more breath and as you exhale center yourself in your loving heart.

When you are ready picture the number five spelled out in red. Allow yourself to feel the relaxation of the red number five.

If you find it difficult to relax, repeat the word CALM, or PEACE in your mind. Give yourself permission to relax.

Next, picture the number four spelled out in orange. Allow your body to become heavy – relaxed.

Focus on your breathing. Inhale relaxation. Exhale tension.

Now picture the number three spelled out in yellow.

If any thoughts come to your mind just observe them and let them go.

Next picture the number two in green.

Scan your body. If there is any tension, gently ask the tension to go away.

Breathe in relaxation and breath out tension.

Now picture the number one spelled out in Blue. As you take in a slow breath and let it out, allow yourself to become fully relaxed.

Begin Visualization

When you are ready, imagine that you are walking in the neighborhood of your youth. As you wander around what do you see? Who do you see?

Allow the sights, sounds and aromas bring you back to a time long forgotten.

This place is alive with activity. Young people are playing the old familiar games. Take a moment to look around you. As you walk down the street you notice a young person sitting all alone. As you walk closer to this person, you realize that it is the younger you.

What is the expression on their face?

How does the younger you react when seeing you?

Take the opportunity now to have a conversation with the younger you. No thinking is required. Simply say whatever comes to mind. And allow them to reply.

Is there anything else you want to say to them?

Is there anything else they want to say to you?

Now it is time for you to leave. Say goodbye to your younger self for now and let them know you will be there for them anytime they want.

With that you slowly begin walking back down the street, leaving your past behind. With a long healing breath, gently bring your awareness back to where you are currently at.

You may want to move your arms and legs around to become more present.

Question: What was that experience like for you?

Question: What were your formative years like?

If you didn't establish an initial bond with a primary caregiver, it can be difficult to bond with others and relationships can be problematic. For this reason, re-parenting work becomes essential, especially for people who never grew up in a loving environment. Re-parenting is not a one-time task. Re-parenting is being the parent to you. Are parents effective when they tell a child something one time or give them only a single hug? Re-parenting is an ongoing daily relationship of love, attention, and support. Throughout your day, make it a priority to interact with your wounded inner child.

Question: How do parents provide love?

This is how you re-parent you. Spend time with you. Make promises to yourself and follow through on them. Give yourself lots of hugs and kisses and praise. Put post-it notes around your home to remind your younger self how wonderful he or she is!

How do parents love children? The top answers are through play, love, and time spent with them. Opposite hand play is designed to address younger age trauma. Do you want to have a little fun?

Opposite-Hand Play

Allow your opposite-hand and opposite-foot to represent the younger you because its play time! Ask your younger self what they want to play and in fulfilling the wishes of your younger self, you bond internally!

Take the time now to have some fun with the younger you. Here are a few fun activities to do with your younger self:

- Painting
- Coloring
- Playing board games
- Putting on make-up
- Bowling
- Ping pong

- Miniature golf
- Darts
- Pool
- Dancing on one foot
- Hop Scotch
- Jump rope
- Soccer
- Skiing (allow the adult and child to interact)
- Cycling (another interaction)
- Tree climbing

As a child, I loved climbing trees. All my childhood friends climbed on a friend's tree for hours! It was only natural, when I started to do reparenting work, to include this into my repertoire.

I took a friend to the batting cage who didn't know how to bat. As a child, he had a problem with his vision and never had the opportunity to play baseball. I showed him how to swing the bat as I had coached and played semi-pro baseball. In no time he was crushing the ball! I mean he was hitting it harder and farther than I was. When he walked out of the cage, I noticed tears streaming down his face. It had been an extremely emotional experience for him, and he confessed it was something he thought he could never do.

After you have done a fun activity with your younger self, continue with the reading.

"Have regular hours for work and play; make each day both useful and pleasant, and prove that you understand the worth of time by employing it well. Then youth will bring few regrets, and life will become a beautiful success." — **Louisa May Alcott**

Stages or Development

Erick Erikson[18] created a developmental model based on our life stages. According to Erikson, people grew up in predictable stages. When they had positive experiences, they had favorable outcomes. If not, it resulted in emotional difficulties.

The first stage of development is the development of Trust. If you experienced trauma or were neglected as an infant, it would result in difficulty with trust.

The next stage pertains to Autonomy. "Is it okay to be me?" This is at the heart of shame and doubt if you suffered difficulties as a toddler. Do you feel like you are innately flawed or should have never been born?

The next stage pertains to Initiative. This describes young children's ability to get motivated and perform tasks. Is it difficult for you getting out of bed?

From mid-childhood to pre-teen, the stage is concerned with Esteem. Do you feel you are just as good as other people? Do you find yourself people pleasing to get your needs met?

In your teenage years, the stage pertains to creating an Identity. Are you gay, straight, male, female, Democratic, Republican, a jock, a nerd? Confusion in this area can cause a person to make radical life choices.

The early adult stage pertains to Intimacy. If you had detriments in your early years, it may be difficult to get into close quarters with somebody when you are a young adult.

Relationships with a developmentally wounded person can be problematic. It can be dominated by jealousy, co-dependency, and abuse.

On the next page is Erickson's Stages of Psychosocial Development.

Stages of Psychosocial Development

Infant
Toddler
Pre-schooler
Grade-schooler
Teenager
Young Adult
Middle-age Adult
Older Adult

Integrity vs Despair

Generativity vs Stagnation

Intimacy vs Isolation

Identity vs Role Confusion

Industry vs Inferiority

Initiative vs Guilt

Autonomy vs Shame & Doubt

Trust vs Mistrust

Increases in Complexity

Proposed by Erik Erikson

We tend to attract people with our same emotional maturity. If you don't trust, it is natural to bond with somebody that mistrusts as well. Addressing early childhood wounds is at the heart of self-helping. We are only as strong as our emotional make up. You can improve the detriments in your emotional make up by opening your heart to the wounded parts inside of you. This is an artform that takes practice to perfect, but it can be established. And yes, this may seem like a big task to accomplish, but it can be simplified when you slow down and make each interaction with your wounded-self heartfelt.

"The most sophisticated people I know - inside they are all children." — **Jim Henson**

Review

- When a traumatic experience is not addressed properly, the mind will regress.
- Spiritual Psychology's revolutionary model, *when love is applied to hurt we heal.*
- Fritz Perls created Gestalt Therapy which addresses unfinished business.
- Opposite-hand writing is a great tool to address unfinished business.
- Object Relations Therapy advocates establishing the parent-child bond.
- Spiritual Psychology advocates establishing your own self-bond.
- We discussed Erik Erickson's stages of development.

Notes:

CHAPTER FOUR: EXPERIENCE

"Turn your wounds into experience." – **Oprah Winfrey**

Being book smart is good but putting your knowledge to the test is a whole different ballgame. Now we start to wade into deeper water. What is your intention for this chapter? Perhaps you might even enjoy the process?

Exercise: Muscle Testing

Muscle testing shows you how interconnected you are physically, mentally, emotionally, and spiritually. You will need another person to help you with this demonstration, so choose a person with an open mind.

When you have found a partner, have them stand directly in front of you. Raise one of your arms to the side and ask them to push your arm down at your wrist and resist them. Tell them to go easy. After they do so, make a mental note on how strong you are.

Next, drop your arm, think about a difficult situation you experienced, and surround yourself in that negative feeling. Next, raise your arm again and ask them to push down on your wrist one more time and again resist them. What was the experience like for you? Did you feel stronger or weaker?

Next, place your hands over your heart and focus on something positive. It might be the birth of a child, someone you love, a favorite pet, a breathtaking scene in nature. Once you have found something uplifting to focus on, surround yourself in that feeling, raise your arm again and ask your partner to push down on your wrist while you resist.

Are you stronger or weaker?

It is eye-opening to realize how the body is affected by emotions. Negativity zaps our strength. With a positive attitude, we are stronger, have more stamina, and are healthier. Candice Pert[19] received a Nobel Prize for proving that when we are positive, the body secrets Neuro-Peptides, which enhance the immune system, slow down the aging process and makes us healthier!

When we have a positive attitude, we are stronger, and it is easier to take extra steps needed to get things done. Getting your mind free of negativity is the next step.

"Suffering is thinking that things should be different from the way they are." – **Dr. Mary Hulnick**

Personal Affirmations

To help keep your mind positive, a "Personal Affirmation" is the perfect tool. An affirmation is an optimistic statement that you repeat over and over to change your belief system. The Human brain hardwires habitual patterns into an automatic pathway. If you find yourself obsessing about the negatives in life, this can become your familiar and hardwired. If you think that you don't deserve to live a good life, this becomes hardwired too. To change a pathway, a different thinking pattern needs to be established. Creating a positive affirmation and repeating it regularly can literally change the way you think and thus create new hardwiring.

How to Create an Affirmation

Compile a list of the qualities you would like to experience more of in your life.

After the list is compiled, choose the top three qualities and plug them into the following format:

I am a _____, _____, and _____
man/woman/ person.

For example:

"I am a safe, positive, and relaxed man."

This is the basic format of the affirmation process. Often, people will create elaborate affirmations that go on and on. However, keep your affirmation simple because you will need to repeat it 100 times a day for a minimum of 32 days. In repeating it so often, it changes the wiring in your brain. After you feel you have achieved what you have been reciting, create a new affirmation.

"I am young, healthy and at peace, joyfully sharing the music of my soul." - **Me**

After repeating your personal affirmation 100 times (which should take you about 20 minutes) continue with the reading.

Mindfulness

"Simple awareness is often curative."

According to Dictionary.com, mindfulness is:

"a technique in which one focuses one's full attention only on the present, experiencing thoughts, feelings, and sensations but not judging them."

To foster mindfulness, practicing loving actions regularly can create an automatic pathway. Be mindful throughout your day.

You can do this while performing the simplest of tasks. Walking, eating, bathing, brushing your hair, or even through dance. When you open your heart during any activity, you are being mindful.

Grounding

I was experiencing tremendous anxiety after I graduated with my master's degree in Spiritual Psychology. I tried using every one of my tools, but they just didn't help. I contacted a teacher and told him about it, who grinned and told me four words - "Go for a walk". After an hour of walking, I felt a tremendous release and I was back to my old self.

The problem I had, was that I wasn't "grounded." When you are working on yourself, it is common to feel a little spacey. Clinically, it is called "Cognitive Dissonance." Cognitive Dissonance basically means the mind is rewiring itself to support a new reality and can make you feel a bit out of sorts. Grounding allows the energy from your head to be transmitted down to your feet and into the earth. This has a calming effect.

Walking and placing your bare feet on the earth are two methods to ground. Here are more:

- Hug a tree
- Hug someone you love
- Take a bath
- Go for a swim
- Get a massage
- Eat red meat
- Drink plenty of water

There is a documentary film called *The Grounded* which describes the benefits of connecting to the healing energy of Mother Earth. Grounding helps reduce blood pressure, improve digestion, assist weight loss, and much more.

Exercise: Grounding

For the next 10 minutes, go outside and place your bare feet on the earth. While doing so, repeat the affirmation you created to ground it into you.

After you have completed the exercise, continue with the reading.

Progressive Relaxation

When your body is relaxed, the blood moves from the muscles and into the areas that need nourishment. There are incredible health benefits to relaxation, and Progressive Relaxation is an excellent method to use.

It has been proven that you cannot be anxious and relaxed at the same time. *"The Relaxation Response,"* a book by Dr. Herbert Benson[20] states,

> *The relaxation response is a physical state of deep rest that changes the physical and emotional responses to stress... and the opposite of the fight or flight response.*

Exercise: Progressive Relaxation

The following exercise takes about 20 minutes. Find a place where you can relax undisturbed for that length of time. You can either sit or lie down. Playing soft nature type music can add a special ambiance.

Progressive Relaxation involves tightening muscle groups, holding that tension in your breath, and when exhaling releasing the tension.

Take in a deep breath and at the same time tighten the muscles in your feet – not so hard as to cause cramping. Keep holding your breath. Now exhale and relax all of the muscles in your feet. Allow your feet to feel heavy.

Choose a word you can focus on to help you become more relaxed, such as "calm" or "peace." Repeat this word in your mind as you inhale relaxation and exhale tension.

Visualize your blood circulating into the tiny places in your feet, bringing with it healing and peace.

Next, allow your attention to move up to your ankles. Take in a deep breath, hold it, and tighten only the muscles in your ankles. Avoid tightening the feet. Hold the tension in your breath and, after a short while, exhale and relax your ankles.

If you have any thoughts, simply observe them, then let them go. If they still remain, visualize each thought being attached to a helium balloon and allow the balloon to float away. With each balloon that floats away, you find yourself becoming more relaxed.

Next, focus your attention on your calf muscles. Take in a deep breath: while holding your breath, tighten your calves, but not so tight as to cause cramping. Feel the tension in your breath, and after a moment exhale and relax the muscles in your calves. Allow your lower legs to become heavy and relaxed.

Next, allow your attention to move to your upper legs. As you inhale, tighten the muscles only in your upper legs. Hold it. Make sure the upper legs are good and tense and when you are ready, exhale and relax your upper leg muscles. Allow your legs to become heavy.

If you are finding it difficult to relax, do not be concerned. It may take a few attempts to master this approach. If you are finding it difficult to relax ask yourself why. What do you think would happen if you let go? Allow this thought to be attached to a balloon and then release it.

Next, allow your attention to move up to your hips. Tighten your hips and buttocks together as you take in a deep breath. Hold the tension within your breath, and after a moment, exhale and relax.

You may begin to feel a tingling sensation in the area you just relaxed. This is the feeling of relaxation. It's what we're working toward.

Next allow your attention to move into two areas: the lower back and stomach. Take in a deep breath and tighten your mid-section. If you have lower back problems, avoid tightening this area too much. Hold the tension in your breath, and after a moment, exhale and relax.

As you allow your stomach and lower back to relax, focus once again on your breathing. Let your body slow down and center itself in the peaceful rhythm of your breathing.

Next, focus your attention on your upper back and chest. Take in a deep breath and tighten these two muscle groups. Hold this breath for a little bit longer, then exhale and relax. If any thoughts or feelings come to mind, simply observe them and let them go. Allow your thoughts to simply move through you.

Next, focus on your shoulders. I like to pull my shoulders up toward my ears for this one. Take in a deep breath and tighten your shoulders. Hold the tension in your breath and after a short while, exhale and relax. Allow your whole torso and legs to grow heavy. Challenge yourself. See how relaxed you can get.

Next, focus your attention on your upper arms. Bend your arms as you take in a deep breath and tighten the muscles only in your upper arms. Hold the tension in your breath, and after a moment, exhale and relax.

Next, focus your attention on your forearms. Try bending your wrists in either direction to tighten the muscles. Now take in a deep breath and tighten the muscles only in your forearms.

When you are ready, exhale and relax.

Now for your hands. You will be making fists. If you have long fingernails, avoid cutting yourself. Try to get your hands good and white as you take in a deep breath and tighten the muscles in your hands. Hold the tension in your breath, hold it, then exhale and relax. Feel the blood returning to your hands. Allow it to soothe and relax the muscles.

Give your hands ample time to recover before continuing.

Next, focus your attention on your neck and throat. Take in a deep breath and tighten the muscles only in this area. Hold the tension in your breath and when you are ready, exhale and relax. Allow your neck and throat to become heavy and relaxed.

Now turn your attention to your face. In working with the jaw, don't tighten the muscles too much. I like to grimace my entire face while tightening the jaw. So gently take in a deep breath and tighten the muscles of your face and jaw. Hold your breath for a moment, and when you're ready, exhale and relax. Now let your face and jaw become heavy and relaxed.

Focus on the muscles in your scalp. Try moving your eyebrows upward for this one. When you are ready, take in a deep breath, tighten the muscles in your scalp, hold the tension in your breath, and then exhale and relax.

Now allow your entire body to become heavy and relaxed. Let the relaxation engulf you. When you feel fully relaxed be gentle with yourself. There is no rush, no emergencies - only a relaxing connection within you. Spend some time with the you underneath the turmoil. This is the real you. Take a minute to appreciate the moment. When you are ready, slowly rise and enjoy your day.

Automatic

How often is your life on automatic? Your behaviors and thoughts may have existed for years. In becoming mindful, you take charge of your life! When a habitual thoughts creeps in, simply observe and befriend them. Later in the book you will learn methods to put the old patterns to rest and create new, more beneficial ones.

Review

- Muscle testing showed you how interconnected the mind, body, and emotions are.
- Affirmations train your mind to think more appropriately.
- Mindfulness is a state of loving being.
- Grounding is useful to calm yourself in the healing process.
- Progressive Relaxation reduces anxiety.
- Avoid living life on automatic.

Notes:

CHAPTER FIVE: THE SUPER EGO

"Enlightenment is ego's ultimate disappointment."
— **Chögyam Trungpa**

Sigmund Freud

An exploration of the mind is a fantastic endeavor because each person is so unique. What makes Psychology such a fascinating profession is what one person believes is the gospel truth, another may think the exact opposite. If an event happens in front of a group of people, each person will have their own version of what took place. Psychologists often wonder if there is an absolute truth?

Sigmund Freud[6], who was the father of psychology, grappled with the functioning of the mind. According to Freud, our mind is comprised of three parts: The Id, The Ego, and The Super Ego. The Id is basically our personality which is like the engine. The Ego deals with reality. The Super Ego is concerned with "defense mechanisms," and harbors our sense of what is wrong or right. The Super Ego is what we are going to focus on right now.

When we experienced difficulties as a child, we coped by creating rules to live by. Fast forward to the future, many of these rules will be outdated because they were created when we lacked life experience. Our task is to discover the rules in the Super Ego that are no longer valid and amend them.

Here are examples of Super Ego rules:

1. *I need to get approval from others or else others don't care about me.*
2. *If you make a mistake, people won't love you.*
3. *Everybody has to follow the rules or else they are reckless.*
4. *If you aren't busy all the time, you are not productive.*

5. *Always put your family first.*
6. *Money is the root of all evil.*
7. *Anger is bad.*
8. *Treat others the way you want them to treat you.*
9. *If you can't work something out on your own, you are a loser.*
10. *You must change yourself to please others.*

The problem with Super Ego rules is believing that everybody 'has to' live their life according to your particular beliefs. However, when you try to control the world, problems tend to follow.

Think about it: Does everybody have to live by your rules?

Instead of trying to control the world, of which you have little impact, why not just try to control yourself? This is all you can do anyway. What you believe is right, is right for you. We don't really know what is right for others.

Here's something to ponder: *What if there was no right and wrong but only learning?*

> *An event is just an event, it is our filters that places a label on it and makes it good or bad; right or wrong.* - **Dr. Ronald Hulnick**

Where did your Super Ego rules come from? Going on an exploration of them can be quite eye opening. To start this process, learning how to own and accept projections become a key.

Projections

Super Ego Rules are underneath every judgment you have. Judgments are the quick evaluations we make. For example: "He's evil." To be honest, when you judge another person, you are really judging yourself. My father even said, "when you point your finger at someone, three fingers are pointing back to you." Sigmund Freud[6] called this process, projections. If your judgment is: "He's evil," what you are really saying is: "I'm evil." When you realize that you are projecting your insecurities onto another person, you can "own" or take ownership of the projection and work on changing your mindset.

Sigmund Freud[6] coined the term 'projection' believing, like a movie projector, we project our negativity onto others. You might think: "She is being judgmental". Well, aren't you the one that is judging her?

Once you 'own a projection', you can find a whole assortment of Super Ego Rules in all shapes and colors that need tending to. This is how the housecleaning begins.

Amending Super Ego Rules

Amending Super Ego Rules can feel like a game. Right off the bat, you can eliminate half of your rules by moving from the general to the specific and individualizing your rules. Instead of focusing on what everybody should do, focus only on what you do.

For example: Change the wording: "Everybody has to_____", to "I choose to_____". In doing this one little thing, you no longer make yourself a victim to what others are doing.

Here are some examples of Amending Ego Rules:

A person is angry with their child.

Judgement: They are a bad parent.

The Rule: All parents must show children love all of the time.

Amended Rule: I choose to be loving to children to the best of

44

my ability.

In this example the rule was changed from 'all parents' to 'I.'

Another example:

A close friend lectures you about your drinking.

>Judgment: He is judging me and trying to control me.

>The Rule: People who tell me what to do are bad and trying to control my life!

>Amended Rule: People who are giving me advice are doing the best they can.

In this example, the skill used is called Re-framing. Re-framing creates a different perspective that is more beneficial. The truth is, we are always doing the best we can.

Another example:

A person enters the express check-out with too many items.

>Judgment: That woman is inconsiderate.

>The Rule: People who don't follow the rules are rude.

>Amended Rule: I choose the follow the rules to the best of my ability and people are doing the best they can.

In this example we again move from the general to more specific. Also, in this example, it is important to remind yourself to ease off your judgments of others to remain calm.

One more example:

A friend's home is messy.

Judgment: My friend is lazy.

The Rule: People who don't keep their home clean don't care about themselves.

Amended Rule: I choose to keep my home clean to the best of my ability. My friend is doing the best she can.

Exercise: Amending Super Ego Rules

Now it's your turn. Jot down some recent reactions you've had to another person, list the judgments and then own the projections.

Next, discover the Super Ego rule that was violated and write that out. Finally, amend the rule.

After you've written out a series of amended rules, congratulate yourself for a job well done.

It can take some practice, but soon you will master this approach.

> *You largely constructed your depression. It wasn't given to you. Therefore, you can deconstruct it. -*
> **Albert Ellis**

Rational Emotive Therapy

When it comes to describing the workings of the mind, it is important to pay homage to Albert Ellis[21]. Dr. Ellis who created Rational Emotive Therapy (RET). RET helps people scrutinize their thinking patterns. Dr Ellis believed that poor consequences resulted from erroneous beliefs and behaviors. He worked with clients to dispute faulty thoughts and behaviors, and then amend them, which resulted in the clients becoming more "Rational."

Dr. Ellis was famous for his ABC model:

A = An *Activating* event is followed by:

B = The *Beliefs* we have about the event and our resulting *Behaviors,*

C = What are the *Consequences* of our Behaviors?

D = If the Consequences are bad, we needed to *Dispute* our Beliefs and change our Behaviors,

E = The *Effect* of doing so made us Rational.

Rational Emotive Therapy is predominantly a mental approach to therapy. It focuses on our belief system. Take a moment to think about a recent upset you've had. This is the *Activating event*. What were your Beliefs and Behaviors? After doing what you did, what were the Consequences?

Amending Super Ego rules is a major component of the Rational Emotive Therapy approach. In changing our rules, we ultimately change our behaviors and become more rational.

A client was arguing with staff then became dangerous. Because of this, the other clients in the room were removed. The unruly client maintained that the staff wasn't hearing her (Activating event). Her belief was "Authority figures that don't listen are bad" (Belief). Her behavior was to get aggressive (Behavior). The consequence of this behavior was having her fellow clients ushered out and her getting kicked out of the program (Consequence). During her discharge, I helped her dispute her belief and behavior, and after doing so, she amended her belief to: "in order to have productive conversations, the message sent needs to be given in a calm way" (Dispute). She apologized and was grateful for learning this lesson (Effect).

Enabling

How much suffering did you go through to learn a life lesson? Since we learn through trial and error, if we don't allow somebody to suffer the consequences of their behaviors, they fail to grow.

It can be difficult watching somebody fumble around with the same troubles that we went through and want to provide them with help. Even if we tell them the proper answer, they still don't listen! This is because people need to have their own experiences. The humbling part is us having to watch from the sidelines.

It becomes tricky when a person you love may experience harm. For example, becoming homeless or getting incarcerated. Do you let them suffer? It is easy to say yes if it isn't somebody you care about it, but with loved ones, it is a different story.

When somebody is not in their right mind, it takes on more critical proportions. The version they have on what is right or what is wrong may be skewed, and if you don't step in, that person may die. In extreme cases, where a person may be dangerous to themselves or others, take prompt action and get the professionals involved.

How to Provide Help Others

To provide help, remain calm. In doing so this will help calm the other person down. Next, really listen. Let the person vent and process their emotions. If they are talking, you are doing a great job. Just be silent and let them purge. The most important action to take is in empowering them. Help them come up with their own solutions. This helps them learn and grow through their own actions.

I often ask myself: am I helping a person in their strength or their weakness? If they come up with a viable plan, assist them to the best of your ability. Remember, we human beings are in this thing together.

"Strong people don't put others down... They lift them up." — **Michael P. Watson**

Review

- How the mind works.
- The rules of the Super Ego.
- We discussed the projection process.
- We explored judgments.
- You learned how to amend Super Ego Rules.
- You learned about the ABCs of Rational Emotive Therapy.
- We discussed enabling.
- We discussed how to provide help to others.

Notes:

CHAPTER SIX: BEING A SUCCESS

"Self-care is never a selfish act - it is simply good stewardship of the only gift I have, the gift I was put on earth to offer others. Anytime we can listen to true self and give the care it requires, we do it not only for ourselves, but for the many others whose lives we touch." — **Parker Palmer**

Behavioral Therapy

Behavioral Therapy was made famous by Ivan Pavlov[22] when he experimented with dogs. He conditioned dogs to salivate when they heard a bell. Behavioral Therapy's key phrase is: "Rewarded behaviors are often repeated". Therefore, as you work on yourself, reward yourself with praise. For example, when you have met a goal remind yourself of it. "Hey, great job! That was fantastic! Normally you would have argued or ran away, but you faced this situation with courage!" Just do so when you are alone, or you may have to defend your behavior.

The 12 Steps of Alcoholics Anonymous is a behavioral approach. Proper behaviors are repeated to create the ultimate reward – sobriety.

Do you want to have a little fun?

The Trash Can Game

Wad up a piece of paper, or use a small Nerf ball, and get ready to play a little game of skill. It involves throwing the ball into a trash can and for you to score as many points as you can.

Here is the point system on sinking a shot: Every step away from trash can equals one point. Two steps equals two, three steps equals three, etc. With each basket, points are added to your score, and with each miss, points are subtracted. Determine where you want to toss the ball from three times in a row, and amass the maximum amount of points.

Strike up the band, and let's get ready to rumble!

When you are ready, take your three shots.

Come on. Stop reading the book and shoot the ball. Humor me.

When done, add up your score.

Well, how did you do?

This is an exercise of goal setting. Did you try a 10-step shot? If so, did you make a single attempt? Many people go after their dreams this way. They go for the long Hail Mary, hoping to make a killing with some scheme and of course wind up falling short.

The ultimate message of this game is to take the closest shot possible because you can make it every time. When you break down a goal into incremental steps, there are a lot of successes that keep moving you forward, plus you feel good in the process.

For example, it took a lot of incremental steps for me to become a doctor. Applying to the University. Buying the books. Reading the books. Attending the classes. Completing the homework. Doing research for the Dissertation. Writing the Dissertation. Getting praise for the Dissertation. Trying to stay humble.

Mapping out a plan of action plays a big part in the behavioral approach.

Reality Therapy

What goals do you have for yourself? More peace in your life? Great health? A new, better-paying job? A new relationship?

William Glasser[23] created the Reality Therapy approach to help people achieve what they wanted by *making a specific workable plan, enacting the plan, returning and evaluating progress*, and *adjusting* the plan when needed. Emotions and symptoms were not considered, but obtaining the proper results were. This mindset is also found in Solution-Focused Therapy[24].

Solution Focused Therapy was a standard approach for servicemen returning from World War II. Because there were too many soldiers to psychoanalyze, a quick approach was developed that focused on achieving goals.

This Solution Focused approach is at the heart of Reality Therapy. Reality Therapy has a focus on the present and an avoidance of discussing systems or complaints. "If it doesn't work, stop doing that, if it does work do more of that" was their slogan. There was a belief that feelings and physiology can be changed, but only if there is a change in thoughts and actions.

As you learned in the recent game, breaking down a goal into incremental steps is important to achieving your goals. The real emphasis in Reality Therapy is creating a simple, easy to follow plan and sticking to it.

How to Create a Reality Therapy Plan of Action

1. Decide what goal you would like to work on.

2. <u>Without making a commitment,</u> create a step-by-step plan, made of "incremental steps" to achieve your desire. Simply jot out your ideas on a piece of paper. Make sure you take into account your physical, mental, emotional, and spiritual levels.

3. When it seems like you have a workable plan ask yourself if you would be willing to commit to doing this plan. If no, amend the plan until you feel comfortable with it.

4. Make a commitment to the plan.

5. After the commitment, create a support group that can assist you.

6. The last step is to adjust the plan when needed. Projects have a way of ebbing and flowing, so keep your action plan updated and flexible.

An Example of a Reality Therapy Action Plan

Goal:

- Be Healthier

Action Plan:

Physical:

- Walk an hour a day. Start by walking at least 10 minutes each day and then increase the time gradually to an hour every day.
- Take supplements daily.
- Eat nutritious food each day.
- Drink water throughout the day.
- Relaxation twice daily.
- Go to regular doctor appointments.

Mental:

- Free-form writing two pages a day to clear head. (To be discussed later in the book)
- Create intentions and recite them on the hour.
- Create an affirmation and repeat it 100 times a day.
- Create an Ideal "Health" Scene. (To be discussed later in the book)

Emotional:

- Opposite-hand write with younger self.
- Opposite-hand play.
- Go through individual therapy once a week.

Spiritual:

- Visualize a healthier body.
- Meditation for 20 minutes a day.
- Ground energy.
- Daily prayer.

Commitment:

- I commit to this plan – it is fantastic!

Support:

- My best friend, my coworkers, and my neighbor.

Go ahead and write out a plan of action of your own. Choose to work on something important to you that you are willing to take immediate action on. Once you have completed the plan, continue reading.

> *"If you fail to plan, you are planning to fail"* –
> **Benjamin Franklin**

Review

- We explored Behavioral Therapy
- We addressed problems on the physical level.

- We had fun with the trash can game.
- You learned about Reality therapy.
- You created a plan of action.

Notes:

CHAPTER SEVEN: INNER ASPECTS

*"I'd heard all the jargon dozens of times ~ the
'alters', the 'personalities' — and dismissed them.
Now they all took on new significance. They were
no longer just words or ideas or theories. They were
people."* — **Kim Noble**

Sub-Personality Work

Have you ever felt like a part of you was running the show? Late
night cravings spells doom for many dieters. A critical voice drives
you crazy. Judging a co-worker for hours on end are just a few
examples of this phenomenon.

According to Neuro-Linguistic Programming[25] (NLP), a sub-
personality can take over the show and direct your life. The addict
sub-personality, for example, can create a living hell if left
unchecked.

Sub-personalities are also referred to aspects of your personality or
basically 'an aspect.' We have hundreds of aspects from strong to
weak who are trying to do something positive to help us out. When
an aspect becomes problematic, NLP has the formula to change it
for the better.

According to Neuro-Linguistic Programming, when an aspect
causes problems, it is trying to be helpful by doing a job that used
to work in the past but now is obsolete. Since an aspect is a part of
us, we cannot get rid of it, but we can upgrade it.

The first step in amending an aspect is discovering what it is trying
to do. This is called 'discovering its positive purpose'. The next
step is negotiating with it. Yes, in this approach you literally talk to
your inner aspects.

The master of this approach was Robin Williams. I used to frequent the Comedy Store when Robin was a budding comedian. He used to give voices to the aspects of his personality but did so as he ran around the room and swung from the rafters. He was the judge, the critic, the people pleaser, the villain, the boss, and even the airplane coming in for a crash landing. It took me days to recover from watching his act.

Here is a list of common aspects:

- The Addict
- The Critic
- The People Pleaser
- Self-Sabotage
- The Judge
- The Prostitute (compromises self for gains)
- The Controller
- The Victim
- The Baby
- The Instigator

You have hundreds of inner aspects and most are functioning well, however, others may be working against the system and need a tune-up.

How to Upgrade an Aspect

1. The first step is describing the aspect.

    Take my "Inner Critic" for example. My Inner Critic is relentless! It reminds me of how I have screwed up things. It critiques how I dress, my hair, my living space, the things I talk about with people, and it is especially active when I am playing guitar to an audience and public speaking.

2.   Next, talk to the aspect and vent your frustration by using the empty chair or opposite-hand writing. For example:

Me: Critic. I am sick and tired of you putting me down! You are in my head all the time and are only focusing on the negatives! I have a lot of positives but they don't count to you. Can't you just shut up and let me be?!

3.   Now let the aspect communicate back.

Aspect: Well, if it wasn't for me, you'd be a nothing! I remind you of what you are doing wrong so you don't repeat it! You dress like a slob and disrespect yourself! Who in the world would want to interact with someone who's hair looks like it was hit by lightning? You are a doctor! Why don't you look or act like it?

Me: Wow! I am tired of your rants! Enough with this! Something has to be done about you. Don't you realize you are a problem? I am tired of your negativity and something needs to be done about it!

4.   Discover its *POSITIVE PURPOSE*. How has the aspect tried to help you?

Me: What's this really all about? Why are you putting me down constantly? What is your positive purpose?

Aspect: I am trying to keep you safe. I don't want you to suffer ridicule from others or miss any opportunities. I have helped you out a lot. The last-minute wardrobe changes and the quick hair fix is from me. I keep you presentable so people will like you and not hurt you.

Me: Wow. So, this is what you're all about. I didn't realize that you were doing this to help me. I thought you hated me. Thanks a lot. I can see you are trying to keep me safe and care about me. That is wonderful, but I need you to do this in a different way for you to really help.

5. Negotiate with the aspect to change its current job duties.

Me: I like the fact that you are trying to keep me safe, but not through negative means. If you know what I am doing wrong, why can't you just tell me what I need to do right without all that negative stuff? No put-downs. Just advise me on the actions that would benefit me. You do this anyway by having me change my clothes and brush my hair. Would you willing to be an advisor instead?

Aspect: Of course I will. Though, I have been getting quick results when I get you mad. But yes, I am willing to advise you in a non-confrontational way. I may not do it all lovey-dovey because it isn't really my nature, but I can ease it back a bit.

6. Have the aspect make a commitment to the new job duties.

Me: Fantastic! Again, the new job is to advise me and ease back from the verbal abuse. Are you making a commitment to do this?

Aspect: Yes I am. And may I say, you did an okay job in our negotiation.

7. Next, give the aspect a new name.

Me: Thanks for the improved comment. At least it is a step forward. Now, a new name is in order for you. Instead of The Critic, how's about me calling you The Advisor?

Aspect: I like it. I thought of myself that way anyway.

8. Finally, thank the Aspect for being willing to work with you.

    <u>Me</u>: Thank you, Advisor, for working with me. I am
    excited to see how our new relationship is going to
    unfold.

    <u>Aspect</u>: Me too.

Exercise: Aspect Work

Now it's your turn. Take this opportunity to work with an aspect of
yours that is problematic. Use the above as a guide and go slowly.
The most important part of this approach is in working with the
aspect's positive purpose.

It generally takes about 20 attempts before you get the hang of this
approach. Please don't worry if it doesn't flow right off the bat.
Eventually, you will get the hang of it and get good results.

> *"Turn down the volume of your negative inner voice*
> *and create a nurturing inner voice to take its place.*
> *When you make a mistake, forgive yourself, learn*
> *from it, and move on instead of obsessing about it.*
> *Equally important, don't allow anyone else to dwell*
> *on your mistakes or shortcomings or to expect*
> *perfection from you."* — **Beverly Enge**

Conflicting Aspects

Psychosynthesis[26,27] was the first psychological approach that dealt
with conflicting aspects. For example, one aspect wanting one
thing and another opposing it. This was also referred to as
"dichotomies." Psychosynthesis was also the first Spiritual
Psychology approach born in the early 1900s. Roberto Assagioli[25]

departed from Freud's belief of sexual motivation and believed more in a person's innate desire to be "whole."

Dichotomies can bog down the system. You may have one aspect that wants to have an intimate relationship but another aspect that wants to keep you safe. This war gets waged underneath the level of our consciousness, but time to time we are all too aware of the internal struggle.

The key to working with dichotomies is giving each opposing aspect a voice and have them work out a compromise.

The original format to do this kind of work was probably different, but I was trained to use the Gestalt empty chair format, where two chairs are set up facing each other. One chair represents one aspect and the other chair represents the other. Now dig in. The real work is about to begin.

Here is an example of this type of work with a person struggling with cigarette smoking.

> *Healthy Aspect: You are harming us. I fear getting lung cancer and heart disease. You know that this is a bad habit. You make me smell. You are running the show and forcing me to do this at all hours of the day! I hate it!*

> *Smoking Aspect: But it calms us down. It gives us a break. We can smell the fresh air. It's how we connect with people. It gives us something to do when life gets boring. It is just who we are. Give up your fight against me. You know you love it.*

> *Healthy Aspect: I don't love it. It is really a disgusting habit. I don't want to be stuck doing this for the rest of our lives. I hate that I get out of breath when I am walking upstairs or exercising. Let's get real, we have to change. We can calm down in other ways, get a break and smell fresh air naturally. What is this really about?*

Smoking Aspect: I am not really happy, to be honest, and I am injuring myself obviously. I am punishing myself on some level.

Healthy Aspect: Well, you are punishing the both of us. I am trying to get better and take care of myself. You are killing us and I want a chance. We've got to work on the sadness together. Don't you want another chance in life?

Smoking Aspect: I can slow it down, I guess. I just don't want stop cold turkey and detox. This is going to be tough. Smoking is my familiar. Sitting down at the end of the day and doing nothing seems bizarre.

Healthy Aspect: Come on already. Don't compromise us. Life is all about making changes and I need you to make a commitment to do this with me. Come on, don't you want us to be healthier?

Smoking Aspect: Alright. Alright. But, let's at least go slowly. I've tried to do the cold turkey thing many times and it was painful. If we are to do this, let's do it the right way and slowly cut back.

Healthy Aspect: Great. Can we start right now?

Smoking Aspect: Sure. I'm just a bit scared of the upcoming cravings.

Healthy Aspect: Let's find out what we can do to ease the cravings in a healthy way. Alright?

Smoking Aspect: Alright. Let's do that.

Healthy Aspect: Thank you for your willingness to change for the better. Just think of all the outdoor activities we can do and the health food we can eat.

Smoking Aspect: What did I get myself into?

This is an abbreviated version of a Psychosynthesis session. This process can be lengthy because aspects really need to buy into to their new duties or else, they will revert to how they were. It is not uncommon in this process for the aspects to come to an impasse. When this happens, agree to disagree and close the session. When you are ready get back into the fray start the process again. Even the most oppositional aspects will eventually meet in the middle.

Exercise: Conflicting Aspects

Now it's your turn. What is something that you are split on? A decision to buy a car, move, remain in a relationship, stay at your job? Use opposite-hand writing or type out a session, like in the example above. Give each opposing aspect a voice and allow them to work things out.

After you are complete, continue with the reading.

Note: I am in the habit of grading "self-counselings". I wish I had the time to go through your writings, but I do have a practice to run. If, you have a particularly nasty aspect that you are trying to deal with and find you are getting nowhere in the process, please email your efforts to me and if I have the opportunity, I will provide you with some feedback.

> *"You have not conquered anyone significant until you conquer yourself."* — **Matshona Dhliwayo**

Review

- You were educated on Neuro-Linguistic Programming
- You learned to work on your sub-personalities.

- You were educated on Psychosynthesis and working with conflicting aspects.

Notes:

CHAPTER EIGHT: EMOTIONAL WELLBEING

"The best and most beautiful things in the world cannot be seen or even touched. They must be felt with the heart" — **Helen Keller**

Now is the time to grab your snorkel and fins. We are going to start swimming in the deep end of the pool. Keep breathing, make sure your younger self has on floaties, and set an intention for smooth waters.

Many people believe that positive thinking is the answer to their problems. This is partially right. We are also emotional beings and are only as strong as our emotional make up. I have a bumper sticker that reads "Inner Child on Board" to remind me each day how important it is to keep my heart open to my younger self. When I keep my younger self happy, I am happy.

We will now start to dabble into your emotions. Each of your emotions are wired into you and are part of the Human experience. Learning how to work with emotions helps you learn, grow, and thrive! We are only as strong as our emotional make-up.

Pain

Dr. Bernie Segal[28], the famous cancer surgeon, wished pain upon everybody. He believed we were motivated by pain. Instead of avoiding it, it's best to just address it right off the bat. Holding in pain or using substances to drown it out only delays the healing process. When you allow yourself to experience pain, you realize it isn't as bad as you imagined.

There are many ways to work with pain. Opposite-hand writing is a great one. Allow your opposite hand to represent pain – don't give it the power of your dominant hand. In utilizing the opposite-hand, it places pain in more of a subservient mode.

Another way to handle pain is through NLP aspect work. Discover its positive purpose and negotiate with it.

In graduate school, we had a pain specialist as a teacher who worked at a top Hospital in Los Angeles. When medication wasn't effective to patients, he was brought in. His technique was to work with a person to discover an off switch. For example, creating a kind of light switch in their mind that they could just switch off.

The human brain is a warehouse of chemicals. We can tap into the chemistry of the brain to treat ourselves with practice. He was a master in teaching others how to do so.

Letter Writing

Letter writing is a quick and easy to use tool to address anger, hurt, and pain. When you are having difficulty, it is important to give it an outlet. Letter writing is a great way to do so. Put pen to paper and express your true feelings. Let that person who bothered you have it! Give them a piece of your mind! Tell off pain! Write in as much detail as you can and when you are complete, rip it up or burn it to release these feelings.

Many people feel they need to send the letter, but why? Is your intention to heal or create more drama? If you received a letter from somebody who was angry with you, how would you react? Do yourself a favor and work only on your side of the fence to bring yourself more closure.

There was a client who was angry with his daughter for various reasons, and after writing a letter, he mailed it to her. The letter only added fuel to the fire and after she read it, it made matters even worse. In him making it important to be right, he may have thought he won the battle, but in all actuality lost the war.

Anger Work

*After being discharged from prison, a client made a
beeline to her father's house then beat him for all the Hell
he put her through in her childhood. She said it felt worse
in doing so because this was an old man and not the
abuser she recalled.*

Anger is an emotion that is wired into everybody. It is there for a
reason. We can work with anger in one of two ways: beneficially
or detrimentally. Detrimentally has us taking out aggression on
others. Beneficially is through alternative methods.

The Gestalt Empty Chair activity is one of the alternative methods.
Putting Dad in the empty chair would be better for all concerned.
In the Gestalt Method, it can feel as if you are confronting the Dad
who did the horrors to you.

Once you get into the proper mind space, let the chair have a piece
of your mind! Physically beating the chair needs to be avoided at
all cost. Anger work of striking objects is not recommended until a
few years of incorporating the Spiritual Psychology approach into
your daily life. In using physical violence before its proper time, it
can threaten your younger self and cause regression.

To get through anger, honor it. Voice it. Write it out and then rip it
up. When we are angry, we don't have access to the higher
functioning of the brain. When anger takes place, all brain activity
shifts to the hindbrain, which is responsible for survival and
instinct.

> *"You can't reason with a crazy person"* – **Joan
> Browne**

The Stomp!

There are numerous tools to help you calm down and get your
mind back in order when anger clouds your judgment. A good one

is listing on a piece of paper everything that is irritating you. Once this is complete, rip the paper up into small pieces, hold the torn pieces in your hand, and on a count of three, toss them into the air with a shout! Scoop it all up and repeat the process until your anger subsides.

Walking with a stomp and forced talking with each step is another great tool.

> "How. Dare. He. Do. That. To. Me! That. Insensitive. Piece. Of. Garbage! Doesn't. He. Know. That. Isn't. Right!"

Get it up and out! Preferably in an area where you can be alone. Refrain from hitting a pillow. The violent act could startle your younger self.

In all actuality, anger is the shield to the hurt that is getting stirred up underneath the surface. After the anger dissipates, interact with that tender part inside of you that is upset.

Opposite-hand writing is another method to deal with anger. Let anger communicate to you in a more civilized way with your non-dominant hand – don't give it the power.

Free-Form Writing

The goal of many psychological approaches is bringing subconscious material to the surface. Free-form writing is the best at doing this. You can use this tool almost anywhere, and it's as simple as writing on paper whatever pops up into your head.

No thinking is required, just allow whatever comes to mind to be scribbled out. Grammar, spelling, and punctuation is not important, but letting the words flow is.

Free-form writing is a great tool to purge yourself of anger. Just scribble out the anger.

If you have repeating thoughts in your mind, it is because a problem wasn't processed properly. Free-form writing downloads these repeating thoughts and helps you release them.

After you are finished writing, rip it up and burn it. Free yourself of all this garbage. If you re-read it, it will bring the subject back to your mind again.

One client used their opposite hand with free-form writing to allow their younger teen to express herself.

> *"A man who has not passed through the inferno of his passions has never overcome them."* - **Carl Jung**

Relationships

Psychology is the science of relationships. When relationships become problematic, it is time to get into the trenches. Relationships bring to the surface our insecurities, fears, and doubts. They mirror back your relationship within yourself to you.

When your relationship is having difficulty, take a step back and observe the situation from a neutral place. Our emotions can paint a picture that isn't accurate, therefore it is important to gather information from a neutral vantage point. The first job at hand is owning projections. The second job is amending outdated rules. The last job is using the opportunity to change yourself for the better.

One of the biggest problems we have in relationships is trying to make somebody change. Making ourselves change is tough enough. Since we have no influence on another person, it is important to make the change ourselves and model the behavior.

> *My grandmother used to say, "When two people meet, they live in a fantasy world. She is a princess who can do no wrong and he is like a knight in shining armor who*

will rescue me. Then the warts start to show, and the real relationship begins. If you still care about the person, warts and all, then it makes a good match."

Relationships help you heal because they trigger your unresolved issues. Once at the surface, incredible growth can take place when you take the time to process through them.

I asked my parents what makes their relationship of over 55 years so successful. My father said, "I know all your mother's buttons and I don't push them". My mother replied, "We make great friends. Each day we make each other laugh and we do things together".

Since relationships reflect your relationship with you, it is important to take great care of yourself. Without filling your battery tank, you have less energy to give to others. Go to the gym. Take the day for you. Have your own life. Continue to actively work on your self-care. In doing so, you are honoring both you and your loved one.

Communication Skills

"A relationship is based on communication". -
John Cena

A relationship is two people relating. Basically, it is all about communication. The strength of a relationship depends on how well each person can communicate when there is a problem. The most important communication skill is silence. Allow your partner to fully speak. Ask them for more information when needed. Knowing your limits is key. If you are grumpy, your partner will get grumpy too. If you are loving, love will reign. When you start to get irritated during their communication. Take a brief time out. Going to the bathroom is one strategy. In the bathroom wash your face and hands and set positive intentions.

A key with communication is having the message sent received. This is the art of communication. Relationships test how well you can hold on to your positive feelings. This is where being stubborn is a good thing. If you can stubbornly hold onto loving feelings, the other person will give up the battle and join you.

Love-based relationships are referred to as Conscious Relationships. In these relationships, each partner takes care of their needs and supports the other. There is a book, *Conscious Loving*, written by Gay and Kathleen Hendricks[29], which helps partners use their relationship as a spiritual journey.

Living in Default

When you fail to set intentions before social interactions, you risk living in "default." This is where you become vulnerable to the intentions of others. People subconsciously are creating intentions all the time, and their intentions can be powerful. Protect yourself from the whims and desires of others. Set the tone for every interaction you have through intention setting. In doing so, you take more control over your life.

Anger – Hurt - Healing

Underneath anger is hurt. Many cut off their hurt and shift to anger, which shields the hurt. When we cut off anger and avoid our hurt, we are stuck in the middle, welcome to the land of anxiety. Compressed, anxiety turns into panic!

Anger

↓

Anxiety

↑

Hurt

Cutting off anger and hurt creates anxiety.

What's underneath the hurt? For many it's too frightening to imagine. Some say they would rather die than deal with their hurt. However, what is underneath hurt is healing.

Millions of people use psychiatric medication to treat anxiety. In numbing out, we avoid emotional healing. Millions self-medicate through drugs and alcohol or distract themselves by staying overly busy. In not addressing the underlying hurt, problems continue to fester. Therefore, it is crucial to be strong, be brave, and make a commitment to the emotional healing process. Keep breathing. You will survive. With a clear intention of being safe, you will glide right through the process of applying love to hurt in order to heal.

♥ → HURT = Healing

When Love is Applied to Hurt, we Heal!

Applying love to hurt is revolutionary! For years psychologists believed that bringing repressed issues to the surface was how people healed. This is partially true. Subconscious material brought to the surface is the first step. Next, we need to befriend it to complete the process.

While working at the Mental Health Urgent Care, we initially tried to have a person look at a traumatizing situation they experienced from as many angles as possible. Basically, the Gestalt method. What was their perspective? What was the perspective of their friend? What was the car's perspective, and what was the perspective of the tree? In doing so, we actually retraumatized people without being aware of it. When we began to have them apply love to the part of them that went through the experience, it showed much better results!

"After a traumatic experience, the human system of self-preservation seems to go onto permanent alert, as if the danger might return at any moment." — **Judith Lewis Herman**

Family Systems

If you think you are enlightened, go home for the holidays. Family has that special ability to go right to your heart. It is a good test to interact with family when you are working on yourself because they serve as such a clear mirror to you. Family interactions provide a lifetime of growth and healing opportunities.

Dr. Murray Bowen[30] created the Family Systems approach which emphasized how families acted like a unit. The nature of a family was to be intensely connected in actions, thinking patterns, and emotions. If one family member changed, it impacted others. Often this change put such a strain on the family that all efforts were made to return that member back to his proper place.
Prepare yourself for this. As you change, people may feel threatened because it causes them to change in reaction to you.

> *Years ago, I counseled a gang member from South Central Los Angeles and after a group he told me he couldn't return to the hood because my counseling softened him. He had become more gentle, compassionate, and loving to himself, and these qualities could get you killed on the street.*

Bowen's Family Systems approach is vast, but has some interesting concepts that may be of interest:

Triangles

A triangle is a three-person relationship system. A two-person system is unstable because it tolerates little tension. But bring in a child, a family member, or a friend, and the relationship is more stable.

Differentiation of Self

Families tremendously affect how members think, feel, and act, but individuals vary in the degree they are comfortable with conforming to the system. The less developed a person's "self" is, the more impact others have on them.

Nuclear Family Emotional Process

How a family adapts to stress shows how healthy the family system is overall.

Marital Conflict

When the spouses get more anxious, each focuses on what is wrong with the other.

Dysfunction in One Spouse

Where one spouse pressures the other to think and act in certain ways, and they accommodate to keep the peace.

Impairment of One or More Children

Spouses will focus their anxieties on one or more of their children - causing the child to act out or internalize family tensions.

Emotional Distance

Where members of a family basically run away from problems.

Dr. Bowen helped clients break free of their family's conditioning and "Individuate" (become their own person). Stress takes place when family members try to conform but haven't bought into the system.

In questioning the system of your family, you begin to scrutinize your belief system. In doing so you consciously decide which rules to keep or discard. If you think you need to change everybody else, think again. Obviously, that is a monstrous task. That's their job to do anyway. The real issue is you changing you and living more in line with your own personal values.

I was at odds with my family and cut myself off from all communication, creating emotional distance during a very dark period in my life. After years, I was invited to Thanksgiving dinner. This was a time that I began to go through therapy. It had been a while since I was accepted by the family and I couldn't be happier. When I arrived, my family was talkative, happy, joking around and I couldn't believe what I was seeing. I confronted them all. "Where's my family? I went through therapy and you've all changed!"

When you make a fundamental change, your demeanor impacts other people and they change too.

"When your mother asks, "Do you want a piece of advice?" it's a mere formality. It doesn't matter if you answer yes or no. You're going to get it anyway." — **Erma Bombeck**

Review

- You learned how to survive deeper waters.
- You were educated on working with anger.
- You learned how free-form writing can help release unwanted thoughts.
- You learned about communication skills.
- You learned the anger, hurt, healing model.
- You learned about the Family Systems approach of Murray Bowen.

Notes:

CHAPTER NINE: SPIRITUALITY 101

The fact that I can plant a seed and it becomes a flower, share a bit of knowledge and it becomes another's, smile at someone and receive a smile in return, are to me continual spiritual exercises. - **Leo Buscaglia**

Let's face it - we are all going to die. Then what? If you don't come to terms with your mortality it can create tremendous anxiety. Coming to terms with your physical death brings incredible peace.

"I'm the one that's got to die when it's time for me to die, so let me live my life the way I want to." — **Jimi Hendrix**

Visualization: Beginning with the Ending in Mind

When you are ready, take in a deep breath and as you exhale, center yourself in your loving heart. Take in one more deep breath, and as you exhale, let go of all the worries and problems of the day.

Picture the number five, of the most vivid red. Breathe in the relaxation of the red number five.

Next, picture the number four, in the color of orange. Allow the orange number four to relax you more, and more.

Give yourself permission to relax and feel at peace.

Next, picture the number three, in the color of yellow. Let the yellow number three relax your internal organs.

Next, picture the number two, in green. Like a bed of grass, allow yourself to be comforted by the green number two.

Lastly, picture the number one, of the most vivid blue. Allow the blue number one to bring you total relaxation.

Imagine you are walking through a spacious park in the country. The sun is high in the sky and wispy clouds are overhead streaming fingers of light to the ground. The beauty is startling.

You are experiencing life in all its splendor. The park has a healthy assortment of trees, plants, and flowers displaying a wide spectrum of colors and shapes.

The air is filled with the scent of fresh cut grass. As you walk along a path, you watch children playing on a nearby soccer field. Their laughter reminds you of the times in your youth when you played with your friends.

As you continue your leisurely walk, the path transitions onto the main street of a small town. Church bells are ringing, and people are entering a church in the middle of town. Curious, you decide to enter the church.

When you enter the church, somebody smiles at you and hands you a pamphlet. As you clutch tightly to it, you notice familiar looking faces as you sit down in an open seat.

This church is magnificent. There are stained glass windows that depict scenes of your life. As the chatter of the crowd subsides, you look at the pamphlet and much to your amazement, you are at a funeral. The funeral is for you.

One by one, people walk up to the podium and talk about

your life.

What are they saying about you?

A person you worked with talks about working day in and day out with you.

A friend talks about your impact on them.

A family member talks about your relationship with them.

A loved one talks about how much you meant to them.

This is the legacy you leave behind.

When everybody is finished, it is time for you to go.

As you filter your way out of the church, everybody's words seem to echo through your mind. Did you have a good life? Did you accomplish what you set out to do? Do you have any regrets?

As you walk back down the main street there is more purpose in each step. Soon the street transitions back to the path through the park and eventually you find yourself back where you began.

This visualization is entitled 'beginning with the ending in mind'. A funeral would be the end and if you work backwards and create new goals and new intentions for yourself, your life can be amazing! Your past intentions brought you your current life. New intentions can bring you a whole new you.

What if you died?

Exercise: Conversation with Death

Using the opposite-hand writing, write out a conversation with Death. Instead of avoiding the issue, go right into it. Give Death the opposite hand and ask it a few questions.

When completed, continue with the reading.

There Still is Time

Life is all about trial and error, learning and growing. If life is a school, our lessons aren't over until we graduate. Bottom line, you still have time to improve yourself. Use everything for your advancement, growth, and development. If there is a problem, face it. When we face a problem and solve it, it make us stronger.

Many avoid failure feeling - "If I don't try, I won't fail". This attitude was very apparent in treatment facilities I've worked at. Patients failed to put in their full effort into their healing because if they tried failed, this would prove that they were losers. When you see failure is part of the learning process, failure means being one step closer to the solution. In giving yourself permission to try, you may actually surprise yourself and heal! Why diminish your opportunities in life? For many, their identity is wrapped up in them having the sick label. This becomes their identity. Why limit yourself? Being an expert and being the victim has brought you to this place in your life. Why not try something different? This takes effort and you are well worth it. Others are happy, why not you? You of all people deserve goodness. This starts with you being good to you.

Failure can be reframed to the learning or growth process. Avoiding this process make you avoid change. The flip side of failure is being a success. Is success really what you are afraid of? If you succeeded, then how would you feel about that?

Many people don't feel they innately deserve success because they feel unworthy and flawed. Love that part. Convince that part inside of you that you are good and have good intentions. We cannot find the Light through the darkness. Identifying with our lack and negativity only brings on more of it. There is time to change yourself fundamentally. It starts with an intention.

God is Love

Spirituality can be a sensitive subject because it is so personal. This chapter presents information gathered through studies and personal experience. Is it the absolute truth? Who knows? Simply check inside of you. If the information touches you in any way, there will be an inner knowing.

> "*Whoever does not love does not know God,*
> *because God is love.*" – **1 John 4:8**

God is Love. When God (love) is applied to hurt, we heal. Spiritual Psychology puts God into action.

> *Then Moses asked God, "Suppose I go to the Israelites and say to them, 'The God of your fathers has sent me to you,' and they ask me, 'What is His name?' What should I tell them?"* **God said to Moses, "I AM WHO I AM. This is what you are to say to the Israelites: 'I AM has sent me to you.'"** – **Exodus 14-15**

When you say - I am - you are putting the power of God into your statement. I am sick - locks in sickness. I am healing - embraces the healing process. I am an alcoholic - locks in alcoholism.

When I started on my spiritual journey, my first teacher was a friend who was much younger than I was, in fact, I used to babysit him. When he was teaching me how to meditate, I followed his instructions, got my legs, arms, and fingers into the perfect position and awaited something, of what I didn't know. There I sat, growing more and more impatient. I judged myself for doing it wrong and stopped abruptly. When I opened my eyes, my friend was grinning at me as if he knew what I was going through. When he told me that he imagines Jesus above him during his meditation I was thrown for a loop. I was Jewish and didn't believe in Jesus but felt that it was worth a try, so I followed suit. In moments I was filled with peace. All the questions I had throughout the day were answered. I was shocked! A whole new world just opened to me. I wanted more!

Meditation gets you in touch with your Higher Self, also referred to as your "wise inner voice". As your internal noise fades, this voice can be heard.

It is important for beginners to know that meditation may flood your mind with all sorts of thoughts at first. This is normal. The subconscious mind is trying to purge itself of all unneeded information. Just let this pass. Soon inner quiet will remain.

Maslow's Hierarchy of Needs

Abraham Maslow[31] was a psychologist with spiritual leanings. He believed people were motivated by a desire to achieve enlightenment. Enlightenment was achieved when basic needs were fulfilled.

Maslow's Hierarchy of Needs

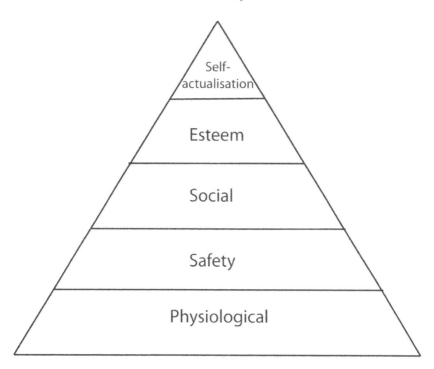

The Hierarchy model starts from the bottom and moves up. When a level is accomplished, it's up to the next.

1. Physiological needs: these are biological requirements for human survival - air, food, drink, shelter, clothing, warmth, sex, sleep.

2. Safety needs: protection from elements, security, order, law, stability, freedom from fear.

3. Love and belongingness needs: we are social in nature and this level is concerned with our feelings of belongingness.

4. Esteem needs: Maslow classified these into two categories: (1) Esteem for oneself (dignity, achievement, mastery, independence)

and (2) the desire for a good reputation or respect from others (e.g., status, prestige).

5. <u>Self-actualization needs:</u> achieving personal potential and self-fulfillment. We are in the constant process of personal growth and having peak experiences. It is a desire "to become everything one is capable of becoming."

If you find yourself on the lower levels of his Hierarchy have patience. It is natural to pursue money if you are poor, or if you are alone, crave a relationship. What is important to understand, is that we are constantly moving up and down on this model. The real issue is how you are with yourself when doing so.

Seeing the Blessings

When we solve a problem, we grow at the level of the soul. Problems that keep repeating, do so for a reason. Spiritually speaking, problems repeat themselves because The God of your Understanding wants you to grow. How long do you want to experience the same problems? Years? Lifetimes? In facing them and working through them, you spiritually grow.

Problems are a blessing because they begin the growth process. After a problem is solved, it is easier to understand what a blessing it had brought you.

Spiritual Beings

> *"We are not human beings having a spiritual experience. We are spiritual beings having a human experience"*. - **Pierre Teilhard de Chardin**

There are no steps or processes we need to go through to achieve spiritual status, we are already spiritual. We are here to help shine our light brighter. In solving an issue, we grow at the level of the soul.

Yin Yang

Yin Yang is represented by a Chinese symbol for balance. Referring to the symbol, one side of the circle represents our shadow (negativity) and the other represents our light (positivity). In balance we are whole. If either side dominates, we are out of balance.

As you work on improving yourself, your growing light threatens the dark, or what we refer to as your "shadow". In repeating your affirmation, it is normal to hear a negative voice within you complain. This is a good sign because it signals you are making improvements. Stay with the affirmation and your entire system will readjust.

In befriending shadow aspects, a lot of healing can take place. You may view the shadow as bad, but it is part of you that has intelligence and motivation. When a shadow aspect says, "No you can't," spring into action. Change the can'ts into cans. There is light in the darkness - it just views issues from a different perspective that all.

Demonic Attacks

Before I lived in a haunted house, I thought ghosts were make believe. The experiences at that house changed my viewpoint drastically. When paranormal experiences take place in a movie, it is just something on a television or movie screen, but when it happens in real life, you feel vulnerable. Learning how to protect yourself becomes key.

> *I rented a house with a few friends and paranormal activity took place from day one. The day we moved in, I was organizing the garage with a friend when suddenly a water bottle resting next to my elbow flew across the room and smashed real hard into the opposite wall. I was shocked! My friend and I looked at each other in amazement. I didn't throw it and neither did he.*

Staying Safe

If you feel as if you are under demonic attack, these thoughts are normal. Many people who are going through difficult times feel that for some reason they are being tested by God or attacked by demons.

Burning Epsom salt and rubbing alcohol in a pan can clear the energy from a room. While you do so, recite a prayer, asking for protection. Sage has been noted by many as a great protector to keep negativity out. Experts advise clearing the room first before applying Sage around windows and doors.

Many believe that crystals also can help. I used to have a nice one in my pocket and held it when I felt threatened.

Others believe candles burns away negativity.

Another way to feel safe is to do something that opens your heart. Dance, listen to uplifting music, watch comedy. Laughter can be the best medicine. A good message to remember is: "The dark can't enter the light."

I worked for years on the evening shift of a luxury treatment facility in Malibu California. There was one evening when every client was spooked and rushed to me for assistance. When I left the staff office, the negativity in the house was palpable. A centering prayer helped calm everybody and put their minds at ease.

Centering Prayer

When a group collectively prays it is extremely powerful. Try to find another person with whom to recite this prayer of protection. Follow along with the wording and hold hands, forming a circle if you have company.

When you are ready, take in a deep breath, exhale, and center yourself in your loving heart. Take in one more breath and as you exhale, let go of all the worries and troubles of the day.

Mother / Father God we ask for you to send down beautiful White Healing Light, for it to surround fill and protect us. We ask that any negativity, any imbalance, any health issue, and anything that no longer serves us be lifted up to the Highest Realms, disbursed there, and return to us in our insight, growth, and healing. We are grateful to be here in Your presence and ask for continued blessings of compassion towards ourselves and others. "And so it is." Or "Amen."

"It is the combination of thought and love which forms the irresistible force of the law of attraction". – **Charles Hammel**

The Law of Attraction

The law of attraction is simply this: "Like energy attracts like energy." Meaning, if you want more love, be more loving. If you want peace, be peaceful. Be careful. If you try to spite somebody this will rebound onto yourself.

Many people block themselves from obtaining their desires because on some level they feel they don't deserve it. We may want to have something, but down deep, a conflicting intention will sabotage it.

"Keep on asking, and you will receive what you ask for. Keep on seeking, and you will find. Keep on knocking, and the door will be opened to you." - **Matthew 7:7**

Ideal Scenes

There is a great formula that Spiritual Psychology uses to attract what you want into your life. It is called the Ideal Scene. First, you need to see yourself in your mind's eye obtaining your desire, and then you need to open yourself up to accepting it. An Ideal Scene combines a series of affirmations under one central topic. Feelings are especially important to include because they magnetize your desire.

You are attracting things into your life all the time. In thinking, "what is the worst thing that can happen?" - you create the worst things. Unlearning this tendency and focusing on the best-case scenarios is how you attract positive things in your life.

Exercise: Creating an Ideal Scene

To create an Ideal Scene, simply have a detailed vision of what you really want. Simply visualize yourself obtaining the desire and then work backwards by creating a series of positive affirmations regarding it.

Here's the process:

- Center yourself in your loving heart – It is important to create through loving kindness.
- Next, set clear and positive intentions.
- Next, visualize yourself achieving your desire and include all of your senses.
- View the example on the next page of an Ideal Scene.
- Enjoy the process.

The example provided on the next page is my Ideal Physical Health Scene.

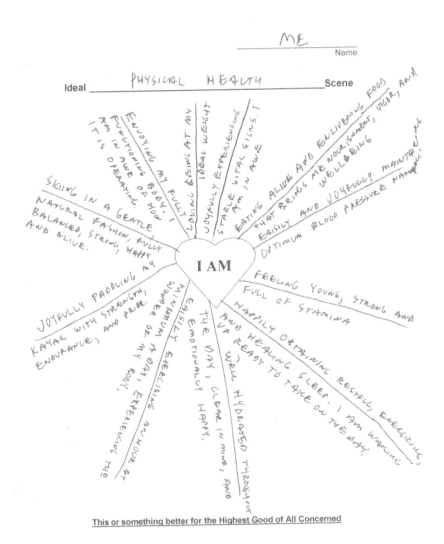

Name: ME

Ideal: PHYSICAL HEALTH Scene

This or something better for the Highest Good of All Concerned

It may be hard to read, so here are the affirmations written down for you.

- *I am loving being at my ideal weight.*

- *I am joyfully experiencing stable vital signs, I am in awe.*

- *I am eating alive and enlivening food that brings me nourishment, vigor, and wellbeing.*

- *I am easily and joyfully maintaining optimum blood pressure naturally.*

- *I am feeling young, strong, and full of stamina.*

- *I am happily obtaining restful, energizing and healing sleep. I am waking up ready to take on the day.*

- *I am well hydrated throughout the day, clear in mind, and emotionally happy.*

- *I am easily exercising an hour at minimum a day. Experiencing the wonder of my body.*

- *I am joyfully paddling my kayak with strength, endurance, and pride.*

- *I am skiing in a gentle, natural fashion, fully balanced, strong, happy, and alive.*

- *I am enjoying my fully functioning body. I am in awe of how it is operating.*

- Ideal Scenes need to have eight to 16 affirmations all related to the topic.
- Notice that all the affirmations are connected to the "I Am" heart in the center of the page. Every statement starts with "I Am."
- Each affirmation needs to have a feeling word or words to attract what you want.
- The affirmations need to be only about your own experience – you cannot create for others.
- At the bottom place the disclaimer: "This or something better for the Highest Good of All Concerned." - You may want

something extra special in your life, but are you open to something even better?

- Make the Ideal Scene 50 percent believable. It is okay to stretch.

There are countless Ideal Scenes you can create. For example:

- Ideal Love Relationship Scene
- Ideal Family Relationship Scene
- Ideal Work Scene
- Ideal Home Environment Scene
- Ideal School / Education Scene
- Ideal Entertainment Scene
- Ideal Vacation Scene
- Ideal Wedding Scene

I created an Ideal Roommate Scene and the roommate became a close friend!

Take the time now to create an Ideal Scene. Plop yourself into a miraculous future. Suddenly you are living your dream! Look around you. What do you see? What do you smell? What do you hear? What do you taste? Then write it out.

Years ago, I needed to sell my condominium and asked one of my best friends, who was a real estate agent, to help me out. We sat down together and created an Ideal Real Estate Selling Scene. When finished, I left the completed Ideal Scene on the floorboard of his car. That Sunday, the condo went up for sale and after few days of a bidding war, mind you in a down market, my place sold for thousands more and for cash! My friend had never experienced anything like that in his 20 plus years in the industry!

After you have completed an Ideal Scene, here are a few suggestions:

- Review it as often as you like.
- Add pictures and items to give it a personal flair.
- Keep it private – this will protect you from having to defend it.
- Write it in the narrative, which is called a "Living Vision". Using the present tense, write down your ultimate future experience.

"There is only one thing that makes a dream impossible to achieve: the fear of failure." — **Paulo Coelho**

Review

- You went on a visualization of your funeral.
- You talked with death.
- You learned about spirituality.
- You were educated on the benefits of meditation.
- Abraham Maslow's Hierarchy of needs model was explained.
- You learned to see problems as blessings.
- You learned we are spiritual beings having a human experience.
- You learned about Yin Yang.
- We talked about how to befriend the shadow.
- We discussed the paranormal and methods to keep you safe.
- You learned about the law of attraction and how to create Ideal Scenes.

Notes:

CHAPTER TEN: QUICK FIRST AID

"Never be in a hurry; do everything quietly and in a calm spirit. Do not lose your inner peace for anything whatsoever, even if your whole world seems upset". - **Saint Francis de Sales**

When you're in a crisis, pause, stop what you are doing, and relax to the best of your ability. Give yourself permission to reschedule your plans because you are more important than items on your to-do list. Simply breathe and above all be compassionate to yourself.

If you find yourself in a crisis regularly, seek professional help. This may indicate a health condition or psychiatric complaint. Taking care of something early creates less long-term anxiety and less havoc on your body, promoting healing.

Quick Solutions

When your system is on high alert, here are some quick go-to solutions:

1. Deep Breathing – Fill your lungs with a series of breaths and oxygenate your system.
2. Drink Water – You may be dehydrated.
3. Go to the Bathroom – Anxiety can stem from intestinal pressure.
4. Ground Yourself - Getting your bare feet on the earth can do wonders.
5. Set Positive Intentions – Your mind can be a powerful healing tool.
6. Recite your Positive Affirmation – Same as above.
7. Break down things into incremental steps – Focus on the task at hand.

8. Interact with your Younger Self – If you don't consciously know what is upsetting you, another part you may, and needs your support.
9. Relaxation Techniques – When your body is calm, stress fades.
10. Meditation – Reconnect with the source of peace.
11. Prayer – Ask for what you want.
12. Gratitude List – Ponder the good things in life - this can shift your focus.

Here are some mainstream approaches that are helpful:

1. Nutrition – Including vitamins, herbs, and homeopathic supplements and juicing. Whole foods can be used as medicine.
2. Acupuncture.
3. Light, Swedish massage.
4. Tai Chi – a slow-motion martial arts dance.
5. Yoga.
6. Psychiatric medication.
7. Sleep.

Sobriety

Drugs and alcohol only intensify problems. They dull the mind, play havoc on the internal organs, and contribute to other life difficulties. This type of cure can be the real cause of the problem. Especially when alcohol is combined with other medication, a synergetic effect takes place that can lead to internal damage.

A person was admitted into the Mental Health Urgent Care Center with severe panic. His medication took up most of my desk! He was taking the maximum dosage of at least 20 prescriptions and our Psychiatrist refused to prescribe anything else to him. I asked him what he was using all the medication to hide from and he answered, "I know, I have gone through a lot of abuse in the past and haven't dealt with it."

Take care of the molehills before they turn into mountains. At the instant you are feeling upset, use your tools. If there is a person in your life that causes you problems, pay attention. Your body and emotions don't lie. Your crisis may be your system telling you to get away from them. Politely excuse yourself and take your inner child out of harm's way.

> *One client told me every time she called her mother, she got put down and felt ashamed. "Then why are you dialing 1-800-MOM ABUSE ME"? I asked.*

Sometimes you must deal with difficult people. Here are some suggestions in order to cope:

1. Set an intention to feel safe, be loving, and a good listener.
2. Repeat your affirmation or use the phrase "God bless you, I love you" internally to keep your heart open.
3. Repeat back what you heard them say. Let the conversation be only about them.
4. Instead of giving them advice, ask them what their next steps are.

> *"Be you, love you. All ways, always."* - **Alexandra Elle**

Person Centered Therapy

One of the best remedies for what is ailing you, is somebody simply listening to you. Dr. Carl Rogers[32] the innovator of the Person-Centered Therapy approach was the master of this. He never gave any advice but rather helped his clients find their own solutions.

People are just as wonderful as sunsets if you let them be. When I look at a sunset, I don't find myself saying, "Soften the orange a bit on the right-hand corner." I don't try to control a sunset. I watch with awe as it unfolds. - **Carl Rogers**

Dr. Rogers believed listening with an open heart was the best way to communicate. There is a book entitled *"Listening is an Act of Love"* that embodies Dr. Rogers' approach.

Dr. Rogers used active listening and repeated back to clients what he heard them say. This demonstrates that what they said was important, and he wanted to make sure that the message they sent was properly received.

It feels good when somebody is interested in what we have to say. Often, clients remark that it's an honor to be with somebody who really gets them.

When there is nobody around and you need to be heard, write. Jot down what is bothering you and come up with an action plan. Then praise yourself for the efforts. Holding something in only makes it fester inside.

A person entered the Mental Health Urgent Care in a crisis, but only spoke Spanish. My Spanish skills were poor, but since our bilingual nurse hadn't arrived to work yet and knowing a little bit of Spanish, I gave her some paperwork to fill out in the meantime.

After I said a few things in Spanish, she said a few things back in English she let it rip! I mean she was rattling off words in Spanish faster than the speed of light! I couldn't keep up. So, I just listened. For 45 minutes she was spitting out tears, snot was running down her face, and she talked like a dam had just burst open! Suddenly the door opened, and our nurse came in to rescue me. After the nurse's interview, the nurse came up to me and said -

"I don't know what you did, but she said you were the greatest therapist she ever had! You really understood what she was going through, and she feels incredibly better." Honestly, I might have said 10 words and didn't understand 98 percent of what she talked about!

Healing takes place when you are in your loving heart. There is no technique, just an open heart. In training interns just out of college, they might be book smart, but the ones who can open their heart and find compassion for a person who is in pain are gifted. I'd rather train somebody with little education and a lot of love, then an incredible student that feels mightier than others for obvious reasons.

I worked with a psychiatric nurse who loved people with Schizophrenia. When a psychotic client entered our clinic, her heart opened wide. You can't teach this. There are natural healers that simply are this way. When I worked with the Spanish speaking client, I just felt compassion for their suffering, and it showed.

Love can melt the hardest heart, heal the wounds of the broken heart and quiet the fears of the anxious heart. - **Malika E Nura**

Unconditional Love

Unconditional love means just that – love without conditions. When you find yourself anxious or depressed or in pain, don't fight it, simply embrace it. There is a part of you that can express love, no matter what the circumstances are. Be kind to yourself when depression hits. Grab a blanket and lay down on the couch with a favorite book. There is a reason you are down and fighting it would help one bit.

When you are anxious, use it as an opportunity to communicate with your scared inner child. In doing this you re-frame the problem as not the entirety of you, but a part of you that is anxious. Now the healing can begin. Communicate through opposite-hand writing or belly holding which is basically placing your dominant hand on your stomach, representing the older you, then hold your stomach with your opposite hand to ally your younger-self to communicate. The belly is the area of the inner child.

As you communicate with the scared part of you, a part of you remains strong and ministers to the hurting part.

Review

- You learned numerous tools to use in a crisis.
- You were educated on the Person Centered Therapy approach by Carl Rogers.
- You learned the importance of unconditional love towards self.

Notes:

CHAPTER ELEVEN: BRINGING IT ALL TOGETHER

"Long you live and high you'll fly and smiles you'll give and tears you'll cry and all you touch and all you see is all your life will ever be." — **Pink Floyd**

Holistic Approach

In learning an all-encompassing approach, it is important to repeat what you are learning throughout each day. The mere fact that your brain hardwires habitual responses, means effort must be taken to change the wiring. Often, people will try a new behavior, feel overwhelmed by repeating the actions after a few efforts, and slip back into the old patterns that got them into trouble in the first place. This needs to be avoided.

In realizing that a holistic approach to change involves mind, body, emotions, and spirit, each effort needs to include them all. Is this a daunting task? Of course it is, but when adhering to this on a regular schedule, the skills and tools you are learning can become second nature.

To stay on task, find a person, or a group to help support you. Alone, we can only go so far but others tend to push us. In our trainings, clients push each other to great heights and soon they are sober, at peace, productive in their lives, and happy.

Is it too much to ask you to repeat your affirmation daily, set intentions throughout the day, reparent the younger part inside of you that went through difficulty, and take time each day to meditate with the God of your understanding? When you schedule time for yourself, even if your day is busy, the results will startle you.

You have it in you to be great and do great things. I have been startled by people whom I didn't think had any hope for success.

Because of this I have total faith in all that enter our program. Roberto Assasioli, years ago believed in a person's innate desire to be whole. People want to heal. I've witnessed people beat incredible odds against themselves. If they can, so can you. That is the amazing thing about us. We are powerful and can direct our power to achieve greatness. You are powerful. You have it within you to be great. Is it easy? Of course not. But you have the strength to do it. All it takes is one incremental step at a time and soon you will arrive.

Please stay on course. You are now fitted with all the tools to achieve what you desire.

The Wall

Take out a piece of paper and list your dreams and aspirations. Let's say a miracle took place and you could have whatever you wanted. What would it be? Make sure to make your desires at least 50 percent believable, but it is okay to stretch.
Go ahead and do this right now. When complete, continue reading.

Once you have your list, on a second sheet of paper, jot down what stops you from achieving your dreams. Make it comprehensive.

When this list is completed, place it on top of your desires list to block it from view.

Suddenly your dreams are out of sight. This is what normally takes place when we allow life's difficulties to stop us. To live your dreams, the bricks walling you off from your dreams must be removed.

What has been stopping you from what you want? The entire list may seem overwhelming, so breaking it down brick by brick can make problem-solving much easier.

Before continuing with the reading, devise strategies for handling the most difficult bricks in your wall.

I always loved this exercise because it reminds me of the

time when I was an intern at a 12-Step inpatient facility in Tarzana California. I asked a group of 40 people what they wanted to achieve in their lives.

One by one, people shouted out what they wanted, and I did my best to write every one of their desires on the chalkboard. Soon the board was filled with some amazing dreams.

Next, I asked the group what stopped them from obtaining this dream. Each person that said something was asked to bring up their chair to represent the difficulty. Soon there was a wall of chairs that blocked the chalkboard.

Oh Lord did the participants want to tear down that wall of chairs, but I wouldn't let them. I was too busy hugging it. I calmly said, "Tear down the wall? But I love my problems. They get my needs met. I get to find out who loves me and who will be there for me. I get housing, food, a relationship, plus an organization of people I get to connect with. If I didn't have my problems, then who would I be?"

It's a big decision to tear down the walls we have built for ourselves. Without the wall, we need to take responsibility, make efforts, stretch our comfort zone, and risk failure.

As the wall remained, people became real. They grappled with risking change or remaining trapped in the familiar. This is what made this job so precious. Helping people in getting out of the mode of just getting by and acting like they think they should versus being truthful with themselves and the group became the mainstay of each workshop.

One by one, as each person renewed their commitment to honor themselves and heal, a chair came down from the

*stack. Soon a chalkboard full of scribbled writing
remained, and everybody celebrated!*

People who are aware of their difficulties and put in the effort to
better themselves are my heroes! This is the road less traveled.

*"Dark times lie ahead of us and there will be a time
when we must choose between what is easy and
what is right." -* **Albus Dumbledore**

Daily Plan of Action

To remain on the road, repeated effort is key. Learning is one
thing: doing moves mountains. Creating a plan of action helps you
to stay on course.

The following are suggestions to include into a daily plan of
action:

Physical

- Exercise
- Medication
- Supplements
- Adequate Sleep
- Relaxation
- Body Work (massage, haircut, manicure)
- Following through on action steps

Mental

- Intention Setting
- Affirmations
- Ideal Scenes

- Owning Projections
- Reframing Limiting Beliefs (Rules)
- Creating a Functional Action Plan
- Free-Form Writing

<u>Emotional</u>

- Self-Counseling
- Gestalt empty chair work
- Inner Aspect Work
- Re-Parenting Exercises
- Opposite-Hand Writing
- Opposite-Hand / Foot Play
- Free-Form Writing
- Applying Love to the Part Inside of You That is Hurt
- Tracking Issues Back to Their Core

<u>Spiritual</u>

- Self-Forgiveness
- Prayer
- Meditation
- Visualization
- Calling in the Light
- Gratitude List

Before you take the time to create your own daily action plan, here is an example of a plan:

"Sobriety Plan of Action"

<u>Physical</u>

- Attend Smart Recovery Meeting once a week
- Attend Individual Therapy once a week
- Attend Group Therapy two times a week

- Exercise a minimum of one hour a day.
- Eat nutritious food and take supplements daily.
- Take prescribed medication.
- Yoga three times a week.

Mental

- Free Form Writing once a week.
- Create and refine Ideal Scenes once a week.
- Recite affirmation 100 times daily.
- Set segment intentions throughout each day.
- Keep an Evening Review (to be discussed).

Emotional

- Complete Self-Counseling once a week,
- Re-parenting exercises daily,
- Self-Praise.
- Opposite-Hand Writing.

Spiritual

- Call in the Light each morning.
- Meditation
- Visualize me being successful.

Support System

- Basic Steps Mental Health Staff,
- Fellow Participants,
- Friends Joe Bo, Collette, Don Ubba, Les, and Adele,
- Smart Recovery People,
- Therapist,
- Church.

After you complete your plan, continue with the reading.

Evening Review

Keep a daily log of the skills you lovingly used on yourself at the end of each day. It will help keep you on track. Jot down how you tended to the Physical, Mental, Emotional, and Spiritual levels.

"Every block of stone has a statue inside it and it is the task of the sculptor to discover it." -
Michelangelo

A Present

Because you have done such a great job, a little present is in order. The following is a visualization exercise. Find an area where you can be relaxed and undisturbed for the next 20 minutes and enjoy.

When you are ready, gently close your eyes, take in a deep breath, and as you exhale, center yourself in your loving heart. Take in one more deep breath, and as you exhale let go of all the worries and problems of the day.

Picture the number five of the most vivid red. Breathe in the relaxation of the red number five and exhale tension.

Next picture the number four in orange. Allow the orange number four to relax you more and more. Inhale relaxation, exhale tension.

Give yourself permission to relax and feel at peace. Scan your body. If you feel any tension just ask for it to leave.

Next, picture the number three in yellow. Let the yellow number three relax your internal organs.

Next, picture the number two in green. Allow yourself to be comforted by the green number two.

And picture the number one in the most vivid blue. Allow the blue number one to bring you total relaxation.

When you are ready, imagine you are walking through your current neighborhood in the early morning. The sun is rising, wispy clouds are high above, and the temperature is perfect for a leisurely stroll. There are sounds that fill the air of birds singing, the wind is lightly blowing through the trees, and the crunch of leaves can be heard under your feet as you walk.

There is a pathway in the neighborhood that you have never seen before. Feeling a little adventurous, you decide to do some exploring. As you walk on this trail, it soon turns into a hiking path. There is a healthy assortment of trees, plants, and flowers of all colors and shapes, proudly displaying their magnificence.

The air is filled with the scent of honeysuckle. You can almost taste its fragrance. Soon the trail follows a stream with water that is so clear you can make out all the tiny pebbles that line its bottom.

Walking seems effortless. It seems as if you could walk forever. You notice squirrels caring for their young. They seem to accept you as you walk close by. Then you notice the trail ends at a cave and you decide to investigate.

As you move some ivy to the side, you notice a wooden door with intricate carvings on it that seem to depict your life. With a little push, the door opens to a huge cavern.

Stained-glass windows allow the light to cascade inside of the cavern, giving it the feeling of a cathedral. There is a marble floor, beautiful Romanesque posts, and to the side are presents stacked from floor to ceiling. Under closer inspection, you notice your name is on every gift!

Welcome to your secret present room. These gifts represent the gifts you haven't given yourself or allowed from others. They have been stockpiled here awaiting you and now you have discovered them.

It's okay to open one up, in fact, do you see that one hopping up and down? Oh, it wants you to open it up desperately. In whatever way you want, go ahead and open this gift from yourself.

What is it? Hold it tight because you get to take it with you.

Your present room is going to always be here anytime you need a little pick me up.

Take one more look around this beautiful place because it is time to go. With that, you find yourself moving back to the intricate door. As you walk through it, it closes automatically.

As you make your way through the ivy, you find yourself back on the trail. As you walk, there seems to be a hop in your step. The present you are holding seems to be a perfect match for what you need.

You walk past the stream and back to the entrance of the hiking trail in no time. Soon you find yourself back in your neighborhood and back to where you currently are.

You may want to move your arms and legs around to become more present.

What present did you give yourself?

This visualization can be used at any time if you need a little pick me up.

Review

- We had a little fun with problem solving.
- Person Centered Therapy by Carl Rogers was discussed.
- You learned how to devise your own plan of action.
- You were led on a visualization exercise.

Notes:

IN CLOSING

"It makes little difference how many university courses or degrees a person may own. If he cannot use words to move an idea from one point to another, his education is incomplete." - **Norman Cousins**

Continuing the Journey

What is taught in this book is a different way of thinking. Many of the rules of your super ego were examined, your emotions were addressed through innovative ways, and maybe you have looked at life in a new way. This can fade and you can slip back into old patterns if you don't continually work on yourself.

For you to continue your journey, go to lectures, attend workshops, attend church, go to therapy, and make time for yourself to simply sit in solitude. Our facility puts on free workshops so consider traveling to Mukilteo Washington for a live version of this information. Many people can be great in the group but bringing this knowledge into their everyday lives can be difficult. It is easy to be spiritual on the mountain top but bringing it into the valley is the ultimate challenge.

"The breezes at dawn have secrets to tell you
Don't go back to sleep!
You must ask for what you really want.
Don't go back to sleep!
People are going back and forth
across the doorsill where the two worlds touch,
The door is round and open
Don't go back to sleep!" - Rumi

Soul Centered Treatment

In the 1950s, Carl Rogers[31], from Person Centered Therapy, foretold of a psychological approach that was concerned with the health of the soul. You just learned the basics of it. Everything happening in your life happens for the education of your soul. Each problem is merely an invitation to grow at the level of the soul. It is up to you to nurture this most sacred part of you.

Now the baton is being passed to you. Share your love, your light, and your wisdom. Be mindful and put your all into whatever you are doing. Living a heart-centered life makes you healthy, strong, joyful, and fun to be with.

When each group finishes a course at our facility, we celebrate the effort they made in improving themselves. During one graduation, one client asked to see the photograph of how they looked upon admit. While viewing the picture they began to sob. They confessed that they were suicidal and decided to give themselves one more chance to live by admitting into the program. They said how eternally grateful they were for doing so.

I will leave you with a couple of stories that have touched my soul. I am changing a few minor details to protect their confidentiality.

Mary

Mary was adopted at birth and from the beginning, she was both physically and sexually abused then given alcohol to drown her cries. From a young age, Mary developed alter personalities. As a young adult, eight alter personalities were vying for control. She coped through substance abuse and self-harm. On her 50th suicide attempt, she put a gun to her head, pulled the trigger and it didn't go off. She took this as a sign from God that she needed to live.

At intake, I learned that Mary had never been in a relationship and was upset with God for giving her such a horrendous family. We bonded rather quickly because all the clients loved me and told her I was safe.

From day one, Mary connected with the Spiritual Psychology approach, especially re-parenting herself. What I will never forget was six months into treatment, she entered my office with a grin. She said, "You won't believe what happened! I looked in the mirror this morning and I said I love you. Then I looked up and I said I love you too God."

Soon afterward, Mary was discharged. She soon found a partner and moved in with him. This was her first love relationship!

A Different Planet

After completing a weekend seminar, of which I nicknamed "The Emotional Enema Experience," I was in an amazing mood. I didn't want to leave, so I helped the staff clean up into the wee hours of the night. Around midnight, I climbed into my car, turned on the news, and the announcer said: "Well if you have been living on a different planet, you'd be surprised to hear that the Washington Redskins have won the Superbowl." I laughed out loud. That was so true. I had been living on another planet!

♪*And in the end, the love you take is equal to the love you make.*♫ – **The Beatles**

ACKNOWLEDGMENTS

"Treat yourself and others with kindness." – **Dr. Noah Young**

A heart felt thank you to BJ Kileen for helping edit this book. Barbara you inspired me and have been a friend for life.

I would like to acknowledge the group of amazing people that have impacted my life. Starting with my family - you have all made a huge impact on me. Mom, you are the best! Dad, I make you out to be a saint to my clients because you are one. My sister Kim is my Guru. Everybody should have a Kimmie in their life.

The creators of the Spiritual Psychology program at the University of Santa Monica - Dr. Ronald and Dr. Mary Hulnick, you changed my life forever. John Whittaker from the University of Santa Monica was there in my special time of need.

Albert Saparoff from the *Get High on Life Program*, you were a goofball and a role model.

Dr. Noah Young, my first and greatest supervisor, you tolerated my naivety and helped me grow as a person. I am proud to call you brother.

Robert Raz and Debra Allen-Seagal from Insight Seminars showed me how I wanted to live my life. Pastor Jack Hayford, you laid an incredible foundation when I was searching for answers.

I need to acknowledge the staff at the Mental Health Urgent Care in Long Beach California. Even though we treated tens of thousands of people, we always found a way to love, support, and entertain ourselves. So, thank you to Dr. Rick Jenkins, Anisa, Aaron, Raz, Anne, Catvy, Susan, Aaron, and especially Myrna Tonic, also referred to as Smyrnacoff, you are an absolute angel.

Thank you to my staff at Basic Steps Mental Health, especially Judith Holtz, Pamela Johnson, and Maria Greene for their dedication, support, and love.

Thank you to the members of the Mukilteo Chamber of Commerce. You have all been an amazing support network.

I want to single out Charles Horowitz. If it weren't for Charles, I would have never been exposed to psychology. His persistence started my amazing journey.

Dr. Joe Wilson and his amazing wife Pam. You are my rocks.

And last, I want to thank the thousands of clients who have humbled me in their dedication to self-improvement. You are truly my heroes.

For more information about Dr. Scott Alpert and Basic Steps Mental Health, go to http://www.basicsteps.life

APPENDIX

[1]Perls, F. (1966). Gestalt Therapy and Human Potentialities: *Explorations in Human Potentialities.* Edited by Herbert A. Otto. Springfield, Illinois: Charles C. Thomas. 35: 1-7.

[1]Perls, F. (1969). *Gestalt Therapy Verbatim.* Lafayette, Ca: Real People Press. pp. 5-108.

[2]Levitsky, Abraham, and Perls, F.S. (1970). The Rules and Games of Gestalt Therapy: *Gestalt Therapy Now,* Edited by Joen Fagan and Irma Lee Shepard. New York: Harper and Row. pp. 140-149.

[3]Passons, W., (1975) Theoretical Components of Gestalt Therapy: *Gestalt Approaches in Counseling,* New York: Holt, Rinehart, and Winston. pp. 11-25.

[4]Kristnamurti, J. (1985) *Krishnamurti's Notebook,* published by Victor Gollancz Ltd. Pp. 1-256.

[5]Hulnick, M. & Hulnick, R. (1986). Various handouts. Copyrighted material, University of Santa Monica, Santa Monica. Adapted by permission.

[6]Freud, S. (1920). *Beyond The Pleasure Principle. The Standard Edition of the Complete Psychological Works of Sigmund Freud.* Ed. James Strachey, Anna Freud, Alix Strachey, Alan Tyson, Angela Richards. Trans. James Strachey et. al. Vol. 18. London: Hogarth Press, c. 1953-1974. 24, 3-64.

[7]Cappaccoine, L. (1988). *The Power of Your Other Hand, Revised Edition: A Course in Channeling the Inner Wisdom of the Right*

[8]Ainsworth, M.D.S. (1967). Infancy in Uganda*: Infant Care and the Growth of Attachment.* Baltimore: John Hopkins University Press. pp. 119-149.

[9]Ainsworth, M. D.S., Blehar, M.C., Waters, E., & Wall, S. (1978). *Patterns of Attachment: A Psychological Study of the Strange Situation.* Hillsdale, N.J.: Erlbaum. Pp. 1–51.

[10]Bacal, H. A., & Newman, K.M. (1990). *Theories of Object Relations: Bridges to Self Psychology*, New York: Columbia Universities Press. pp. 29-66.

[11]Bowlby, J., & Ainsworth, M. D. (1991). *An Ethological Approach to Personality Development. American Psychologist.* 46,333-341.

[12]Cassidy, J. & Shaver, P. (1999). *Handbook of Attachment: Theory, Research, and Clinical Applications*, New York: Guilford Press. pp. 8-83.

[13]Firestone, R. (1987). *The Fantasy Bond: Effects of Psychological Defenses on Interpersonal Relations.* New York: Human Sciences Press. pp. 35-43.

[14]Karen, R. (1994). *Becoming Attached: First Relationships and How They Shape Our Capacity to Love.* Oxford University Press, Inc. pp.146-164.

[15]Klein, M. (1950). *Writings of Melanie Klein 1921 – 1945 Contributions to Psycho-Analysis*: 1921-1945 / with an introduction by Ernest Jones, London: Hogarth Press. pp. 25-80, 104-117, 210-218.

[16]Spillius, E. B. (1988). *Melanie Klein Today, Developments in Theory and Practice,* Vol. 2, Mainly Theory, London: Routledge Press. pp. 17-21.

[17]Winnicott, D. (1960). The Theory of the Parent-Child Relationship, *International Journal of Psychoanalysis.* 41:585-595.

[17]Winnicott, D. (1953). Transitional Objects and Transitional Phenomena: *International Journal of Psychoanalysis*, 34:89-97.

[17]Winnicott, D.W. (1945). Primitive Emotional Development. *International Journal of Psychoanalysis*, 26:137-143.

[17]Winnicott, D.W. (1965). *The Maturational Processes and the Facilitating Environment*, London: IUP, Hogarth Press. pp. 37-56.

[18]Erikson, E.H. (1963). Eight Ages of Man: *Childhood and Society*, 2nd edition. New York: Norton. pp. 247-274.

[19]*Pert C.B, Snyder S.H. (March 1973). "Opiate receptor: demonstration in nervous tissue". Science. 179 (4077): 1011–4. doi:10.1126/science.179.4077.1011. PMID 4687585*

[20]Benson, H. (1977). *The Relaxation Response*, New York: William Morrow and Company, Inc. p.114

[21]Ellis, A. (1962). *Reason and Emotion in Psychotherapy: A Comprehensive Method of Treating Human Disturbances.* Citadel, pp. 8-479.

[22]*Pavlov I.P., (1960) [1927]. Conditional Reflexes. New York: Dover Publications.* (the 1960 edition is not an unaltered republication of the 1927 translation by Oxford University Press)

[23]Glasser, W. (1975). *Reality Therapy,* New York: Harper and Row. pp. 5-74.

[24]De Shazer, S. & Kim Berg I. (1995). *The Brief Therapy Tradition.* In: John H. Weakland, and Wendel A. Ray (eds.) *Propagations: Thirty Years of Influence From the Mental Research Institute.* Binghamton, NY: The Haworth Press, pp. 249–252.

[25]Bandler, R., & Grinder, J. (1982). *Reframing: Neuro-Linguistic Programming and the Transformation of Meaning*, Utah: Real

People Press. pp. 45-63, 102-115, 179.

[26]Assagioli, R. (1965). *Psychosynthesis, a Manual of Principles and Techniques,* New York: Hobbs, Doorman & Company. pp.1-23.

[27]Ferrucci, P. (1982). *What We May Be: Techniques for Psychological and Spiritual Growth Through Psychosynthesis*, New York: G. P. Putnam's Sons. pp. 43-46, 59-73.

[28]Segal, B. (1986). *Love, Medicine & Miracles* – Harper Collins Publishers pp. 3-243

[29]Hendricks, G.& K (1992) *Conscious Loving: The Journey to Co-Commitment*, New York: Bantam Books. Pp. 3-304.

[30]Bowen, M. (1978), *Family Therapy in Clinical Practice*, Northvale, NJ: Jason Aronson Inc.,

[31]Maslow, A. (1943). *A Theory of Human Motivation. Psychological Review, 50(4)*, 370-96.

[32]Rogers, C. (1959). Formulations of the Person and the Social Context. *Psychology: A Study of Science.* vol. 3, New York: McGraw Hill. pp. 184-256.

[32]Rogers, C. (1980). *A Way of Being* Boston: Houghton Mifflin Co. pp. 6-282.

ABOUT THE AUTHOR

Scott Alpert is a Doctor of Clinical Psychology specializing in the discipline of Spiritual Psychology. Dr. Alpert has 25 years of field experience. He has supervised mental health and chemical dependency Interns for over ten years. He is the owner / operator of Basic Steps Mental Health, an outpatient clinic located in Mukilteo Washington and provides Intensive treatment to people suffering from mental illness and substance abuse problems. He also treats people simply wanting self-improvement.

Dr. Alpert worked at the first Mental Health Urgent Care Center in the United States where he treated over 7.000 people in crisis. He has worked with many different populations from the homeless to entertainers known throughout the world.

Dr. Alpert in 2013 co-founded a Residential treatment facility and in 2017 opened his own Outpatient clinic for more community access.

Dr. Alpert has written two books *Crisis Management: Step by Step* and *The Burn Ward: A Party Animal's road to Enlightenment*. He has appeared on national Radio, he is an avid blogger, he is a lecturer, and Dr Alpert is an advocate of alternative methods of treatment. Dr. Alpert has one mission – spreading the word of Spiritual Psychology.